PIONEER CONSERVATIONISTS OF WESTERN AMERICA

Peter Wild

Introduction by Edward Abbey

MOUNTAIN PRESS PUBLISHING COMPANY

MISSOULA 1979

Parts of this book first appeared
in somewhat different form
in *High Country News.*

© Copyright 1979
Mountain Press Publishing Co.

Library of Congress Cataloging in Publication Data

Wild, Peter.
   Pioneer conservationists of western America.

   Bibliography: p.
   Includes index.
   1. Conservationists—The West—Biography. 2. The
West—Biography. I. Title.
S926.A2W54   333.7'2'0922 [B]   78-15042
ISBN 0-87842-107-6

MOUNTAIN PRESS PUBLISHING COMPANY
MISSOULA, MONTANA

For Wallace Stegner

who, through his comprehension and
sympathy, has helped others
understand the American West.

ALSO BY PETER WILD

CHIHUAHUA

THE CLONING

COCHISE

NEW AND SELECTED POEMS

WILD'S MAGICAL BOOK OF CRANIAL EFFUSIONS

PELIGROS

TERMS AND RENEWALS

FAT MAN POEMS

THE AFTERNOON IN DISMAY

Contents

viii

Illustrations

x

Preface

It is heartening to see the growing interest in the figures who have made care for the earth an essential issue in our lives. They are, as it happens, some of the most compelling and colorful personalities the nation has produced. The recent surge of books and articles about them reflects not only Americans' impulse to live more in harmony with their delicate planet but also the desire to explore the roots, to understand the founders, of their present concerns. This book is part of that trend, an effort to make the personalities and accomplishments of the major conservation figures of the American West more widely accessible. It came about when Jim Maguire of Boise State University suggested to the editors of *High Country News* that the environmental newspaper run a series on Western conservationists, both past and present. I was delighted when Joan Nice asked me to write the pieces, if for no other reason than it provided an excuse for further study of the men and women of the West who most fascinated me, those who, armed with considerable foresight and concern for the West's future, set out to develop alternatives to the country's often thoughtless approaches to its land. Collectively, they formulated a broad and positive ethic of care, one that we are beginning to realize is essential, not only to our prosperity, but to our very survival on an abused and finite planet.

The project presented some interesting problems. First of all, who belonged in such a study? Secondly, was there a common factor other than their various interests in conservation that brought the diverse personalities together in the context of the West?

As to the first problem, certain well-known figures — John Muir, Gifford Pinchot, and Aldo Leopold — were of obvious importance, and many others quickly presented themselves. Faced with a wealth of possibilities, I turned to Western historians, conservationists, and scientists, and bluntly asked one question: Who are the West's most significant figures, the movers and shakers of conservation? They responded with a variety of enthusiastic choices, each justified in one way or another. Yet a core group of names kept appearing on their lists. Always somewhat leery of truth by consensus, I pondered their counsel, then took on the responsibility of making the final choices myself, though comforted that, as it turns out, the selection is backed by a certain solidarity of opinion. Inevitably, people will come to mind — Robert Marshall, Howard Zahniser, and Arthur Carhart — who played important roles in the developing environmental movement and who well might have been included. The fact that they are not discussed here in detail is no comment on their contributions. Rather, the figures in this book were chosen with the idea that they represent various aspects of a cause larger than themselves, one that touches on a host of other concerned and significant individuals.

Conservation was not effective until it became a

nationwide movement. Yet it began and is sustained by individuals of exceptional vision and strength. Their personalities are as diverse as their specialties: forestry, history, wildlife, literature, politics, drama, and, in at least a couple of the cases represented here, all-round Ezekiel of the American scene. Much of this book necessarily deals with the founding of government agencies, changing laws, and the general sweep of American history as they bear on conservation as it is today. However, more than anything else this book is about how the shapes of personalities in turn shaped contributions to environmental reforms. The bibliography points the reader toward further exploration.

Many of the figures spent much of their lives outside the West. John Muir was born in Scotland, Mary Austin grew up in the Midwest, and Joseph Wood Krutch earned his first fame as a scholar and critic in New York City — a diversity typical of a growing region where at times everyone seems to be from somewhere else. Nevertheless, without exception the focus of their environmental hopes was on the West, and they looked to the Western United States as a place to put their ideas into practice.

That was at least part of the answer to the conundrum concerning a unifying factor. A glance at a map will show that by far most National Parks, National Forests, and similar reserves are West of the Mississippi. And with good reason. The East produced noble voices — Thoreau, George Perkins Marsh, and John Burroughs — for saner approaches to our natural heritage. However, it was only in the West, when the nation reached the end of the continent and realized that both beauty and needed resources were exhaustible, that conservation became an urgent cause with large and tangible results. Hence, one of the major themes found here: the American West as the birthplace of the present conservation movement.

A word needs to be said about the title of this book. The term "pioneer" brings to mind the rawboned trailblazer conquering nature in the struggle to make a living in the wilderness. At first thought it would seem appropriate to a study of those who attempted to protect the land from the destruction that accompanied the opening of the West. Yet conservationists were, and still are, in the essence of the word discoverers, not necessarily of new lands but of new ways of seeing the earth, of a new, more harmonious ethic toward it. David Brower has said that, "The miracle of soil, alive and giving life, lies thin on the only earth, for which there is no spare. We seek a renewed stirring of love for that earth.... We believe there is still time for a rewarding renaissance. The old one came with discovery of new lands to exploit. The new one comes with discovery of the earth's limits." Almost daily we are reminded of the consequences of past and present mistakes—pollution, shortages of food, energy, and water, even space—as the earth nears its limits. In this sense, as explorers daring to strike out on more enlightened and long-term approaches to living on the planet, conservationists are true pioneers — as much and more so perhaps as were their fathers.

Peter Wild
Tucson, Arizona
December, 1978

Acknowledgments

Many people helped make this book possible, and, though I can not thank all of them individually here, I would like to mention a few by name, with the qualification that any errors of fact or judgment found in the following pages are entirely my own.

Those who offered encouragement and detailed suggestions as to the scope of the book include Michael McCloskey, Executive Director of the Sierra Club; Hal Coss, Biologist, Saguaro National Monument; Frank Graham, Jr., Field Editor of *Audubon;* Howard E. Weaver, of the Association of Interpretive Naturalists; Wallace Stegner; Edward Abbey; Robert Craig, General Curator, the Arizona-Sonora Desert Museum; Frances Gendlin, Editor, *Sierra: The Sierra Club Bulletin;* Roxanna Sayre, Senior Editor, *Audubon;* Margaret Murie; Juel Rodack, Chairman, Arizonans for Quality Environment; and Mr. and Mrs. Ernest Youens.

Officials of the Wilderness Society were especially generous with their time and knowledge: Clifton Merritt, Deputy Director; Michael Nadel, Special Consultant to the Executive Director; James G. Deane, Editor of the Society's publication, *The Living Wilderness;* Sally Ranney, Resource Policy Analyst; and David Foreman, Southwest Representative.

Joan Nice, Editor of *High Country News,* provided not only friendship and sound suggestions, but also searched out many of the photographs included here. My warmest thanks to her and her enthusiastic staff. I further appreciate the guidance of her husband Bruce Hamilton,

Sierra Club Representive for Wyoming and the Northern Great Plains.

Mrs. Joseph Wood Krutch helped with fresh insights on her husband's life in New York and details of his delight in America's deserts. I remember her not only for her kindness but for her savory Basque stew. Jeff Gailiun, from his lookout in Kanab, Utah, passed on information on Edward Abbey country.

A number of colleagues at the University of Arizona steered me straight where otherwise I would have gone wrong. Professors Arthur Kay and John McElroy gave of their time and special knowledge of American literature as if the project were their own, and Pat Paylore, Assistant Director of Arid Lands, provided expert information on Western deserts.

I should also like to thank Pat White, a secretary in the Department of English at the University of Arizona, and Peggy Shumaker, a graduate student; they helped make preparation of the manuscript a pleasant task.

Librarians responded to my questions with a kindness and interest far beyond the scope of their duties. To me they are a special breed, and I want to assure this particularly to the following: Charles Peters, Lois Olsrud, Phyllis Ball, and Mirene Hazebrouck, all of the University of Arizona Library; also Betty Anderson, Assistant Librarian, Estes Park Public Library, and Eleanor M. Gehres of the Denver Public Library Western History Department. Both Rolene Britson of the Iowa State Historical Department and Elizabeth Johnson of the State Library Commission of Iowa searched their holdings for important but obscure documents relating to Enos Mills.

I want to thank my wife Sylvia for her encouragement and enduring patience.

Lastly, I thank a young woman who cheerfully and repeatedly let me slip into a library during the dim morning hours, long before it officially opened.

Introduction by
Edward Abbey

If, as some believe, the evolution of humankind is the means by which the world of nature has become conscious of itself, then it may well follow that the environmentalist cause may be the late-flowering conscience of that consciousness. A vainglorious exaggeration? Not at all, if in environmentalism we can see a logical extension of the traditional Christian ethic — and that of the other world religions — beyond the narrowly human to include the living creatures that share this planet with us, not only those obviously beneficial to us but even those which appear to be competitors and enemies. Nor does the broadening of the ethic stop at this point. Once we become generous enough in spirit to share good will with all living things we can proceed from there to the non-living, the inorganic, to the springs, streams, lakes, rivers and oceans, to the winds and clouds and the air, to the very rocks which form the foundation of the land, of the hills, mountains, swamps, deserts, plains and seashores that provide sustenance for our bodily lives and, equally important, delight to our souls.

All is one, say the seers. Well, maybe. Some of us might

prefer to stress the unique, the individual, the diversity of things. But no thinking person can deny any longer that all things, animate and inanimate, living and (as we say) non-living, are clearly interdependent. Each form of life needs the others. We see ourselves, the human race, as the apex of a pyramid of life, the point of it all — and not without justice. Through humanity the earth finds its voice. But we in turn are merely raw material for others; the micro-organisms that thrive in our bloodstreams and intestines while we live, the bacteria that feast on our flesh after death, the plants that draw nutriment from our bones could all be entitled to believe from their point of view that God created the human race to serve their needs. The very concept of a special creation should give pause to those Christians who hold the view, still widespread and dominant in our society, that everything on earth exists for the sake of man.

This is not to say that the Peaceable Kingdom can or ever should be established on earth. Conflict between species is inevitable, necessary and, up to an optimum point, desirable. When the lion lies down with the lamb it must be for the purpose of sharing a dinner, a dinner in which one eats and one is eaten. Otherwise, the lion would starve to death. The lamb itself eats grass, tender, delicate and living beings with who knows what fine emotions and refined aspirations of their own? The moralistic vegetarian is a hypocrite; no self-respecting herbivore would share such a doctrine for a moment.

Competition within the species is likewise desirable — to a point. An absolute leveling of men and women would reduce humankind to the status of the social insects; good enough for ants, bees and termites but inappropriate to our kind and a serious injustice to all with those special qualities and abilities which give variety, vigor, zest, progress (yes, there is such a thing as progress) and finally glory to the human enterprise. Any Utopia, any Golden

Age of Unlimited Power and Plenty, whether mythical or pastoral or technological, where the needs and pleasures of life can be obtained without effort, would be a world of insufferable boredom, degrading humans to the sloth and torpor of swine in a luxury sty; unworthy of us, the death of our nature.

Nevertheless the opposite course leads to an equally fatal result. Unlimited struggle within a species would destroy that species; the human race has reached a stage in its cleverness where, for example, we can continue to have war, or science, but no longer both. Nor are we wrong to strive for justice within society, for the fair division of wealth, for charity toward the weak, the old, the foolish. ("Stand up for the stupid and crazy," said Whitman.) Each has something to contribute toward the whole; the mad may be saints, the crippled may be artists, magicians, craftsmen. Human society is based on mutual aid, cooperation, sharing — without those attributes it would perish. What the conscience of our race — environmentalism — is trying now to tell us is that we must offer to other forms of life and to the planet itself the same generosity and tolerance that we require from our fellow humans. Not out of charity alone — though that is reason enough — but for the sake of our own survival as free men and women. Certainly the exact limits of what we can take and what we must give are extremely hard to determine; few things can be more difficult than attempting to measure our needs, to find that optimum point of human population, human development, human industry, beyond which the returns begin to diminish. Very difficult; but the chief difference between humankind and the other animals is the ability to observe, think, reason, experiment, and communicate with one another through language; the mind is our proudest distinction, the finest gift and achievement of our evolution. I think we may safely assume that we are meant to use it.

What are the alternatives to reason and the conservationist conscience? There seems to be only one: go on as we are going now, submitting to the blind drift of human domination over the planet, the mindless growth in population, the greed and gluttony of the rich nations, the ever-more desperate needs of the poor, leading in turn to one of two most probable resolutions of an ever-increasing web of difficulties:

First, an intensification of the conflicts within each nation and among the nations as the scramble for dwindling natural resources becomes more severe. We can see early symptoms of this conflict in the United States, where industrialists have begun to recognize conservationists and environmentalists — not labor leaders, not Marxists — as their chief antagonists in determining the character of the American future. In fact business leaders have succeeded already in creating hostility between organized labor and the environmental movement; one of the most important tasks for environmentalists in the near future will be the reversal of that trend, convincing working people (and almost all of us belong to that class) that their own best interests, their health, livelihoods, happiness, lie in supporting not opposing labor-intensive rather than capital-intensive, basically agrarian rather than industrial, steady-state rather than ever-expanding economy. Civilization, if we are ever to achieve it, will be based on a mature, stabilized political economy which functions so smoothly that, as with internal bodily functions, we can take its health for granted and become aware of pain only when something is going wrong. The growth-economy, contrary to the belief of many, is the enemy of a healthy human culture and an obstacle to the realization of that free, green, wide-open and spacious form of human society which alone deserves the honor of the title "civilization." Complex matters, indeed; but no one ever said it would be easy. All things excellent, said Spinoza, are as difficult as they are rare.

Assuming however that efforts at internal reconcilia-
tion fail, that the environmental movement fails, we will
see conflicts increase, becoming more bitter as classes,
factions, ethnic groups and races compete with one
another for as much as each can take from what economic
wealth remains available in North America. In the process of the struggle such luxuries as wilderness and wildlife, public lands and physical freedoms will soon vanish,
as they have already largely vanished from Europe, Asia,
Africa and South America. At the same time the competition among the nations will drive all closer to the edge of
war, every nation seeking to promote its own economic
growth in the only way it can, that is, at the expense of
other nations. The result will be, as history demonstrates
over and over again, war and civil war, accompanied by
famine, plague and the descent, once again into another
Dark Age. If — the big *if* that haunts humanity today — if
enough of a human population survives nuclear, biological and chemical warfare to make any kind of human
history still plausible.

So much for the familiar and popular disaster
hypothesis. The second possible "solution" to the difficulties posed by unlimited population growth and insatiable
industrial growth would be the creation of a planetary
technocracy, a technological superstate in which we sur-
render our individual desires and personal liberties to
some kind of international, computerized, scientifically-
engineered, nuclear-powered despotism administrated,
no doubt, by such visionaries as R. Buckminster Fuller,
Herman Kahn, Glenn T. Seaborg, and their many counterparts in the other industrialized nations. In a global
order combining the best features of Huxley's *Brave New
World,* Orwell's *1984,* and Stanislaw Lem's *The
Futurological Congress,* we can foresee the transforma-
tion of Spaceship Earth into an orbiting food machine,

automatically processing rock, seawater, garbage, sewage, air into vitamin enriched snack packs for a population of 40 billion drug-pacified, comatose, semi-human inhabitants. The prophets of technology say it can be done; and if it can be done then, by their way of thinking, it should, must and will be done. But who wants to live in their world? Survival alone is not enough; we demand survival with dignity, liberty and honor.

Commonplace nightmares. Perhaps we will find a way to muddle through and between the gruesome horns of our awesome dilemma. If we do, I think we will owe more than we can measure to the thinking of such people as Peter Wild writes about in this book, to his little band of pioneer conservationists who have done so much to offer us alternatives to the Expand or Expire theory of human endeavor. Mr. Wild has deliberately limited his subject to the lives and work of a few modern Americans whose chief concern has been an effort at saving the American West from the rapacity of the industrial way of death, but this limitation is quite natural. The American West (including Alaska) is one of the few places left on earth where it is still feasible to make a stand against the zeal of the Growth Fanatics, the graph-paper mentality of the GNP economists, the replenish-and-forever-multiply theology of the American Yahoo Church — all of the descendants of those hordes of avaricious peasants (our forefathers) who swarmed across the Atlantic to fall, like a plague of locusts, upon the sweet, lovely, defenseless virgin lands of America. All of them. All of us.

In any case, the American West offers what may be our final opportunity to save a useful sample of the original America. It is not merely a question, however, of preserving forests and rivers, wildlife and wilderness, but also of keeping alive a certain way of human life, the wholesome and reasonable balance between industrialism and agrarianism, between cities and small towns, between private property and public property, that makes the American West so desirable a place to live. Here it is still possible to enjoy the advantages of contemporary technological culture (to call this regime a "civilization" would be, in my sense of the word, an exaggeration) without having to endure so much of the overcrowding and consequent filth, strife, stress characteristic of this culture in less fortunate regions. If we can draw the line against the industrial machine in the West, and make it hold, then perhaps in the decades to come we can gradually force industry underground, where it belongs, and restore to the other parts of our nation their rightful heritage of breathable air, drinkable water, a democratic industrialism and a decentralized agriculture. Finally and maybe most important—we can provide for every man, woman and child sufficient open space to make possible the fullest realization of human freedom. What good is a Bill of Rights that does not imply the right to play, to wander, to stillness and solitude, to discovery and physical adventure? —

Ah well, we live, as Dr. Johnson said, from hope to hope. In this book, through his study of a group of Americans who present a new way of looking at the relationship between humankind and the natural world, Peter Wild offers grounds for hope. Hope for a new beginning. But only a beginning. It will be the job of the next generation of thinkers and doers to keep that hope viable and bring it closer to reality. If successful they may succeed in making America, not the master of the earth (a trivial and now impossible goal), but rather an example to all nations of what is possible. Was that not the whole point and purpose of the American adventure?

Edward Abbey

At the end of the open road we come to ourselves.

—Louis Simpson

John Muir, Scottish immigrant, inventor, wanderer. Foremost spokesman for preserving the American West. State Historical Society of Wisconsin.

Chapter 1

Visions and Revisions: Conservation Begins in the American West

At the end of the open road we come to ourselves.
—Louis Simpson

"Ocian in view! O! the joy," shouted Captain William Clark into the fog. Together with Meriwether Lewis and their little band, he had just ended an eighteen-month search for the Pacific. They had rowed and shoved their boats up the Missouri River, crossed virgin plains, nearly frozen and starved in Idaho's Bitterroot Mountains. Then, sensing the end of their journey, they glided down the vast and misty Columbia River to the ocean. It was a dramatic moment, the first time an expedition from the United States had crossed the continent.

It was also one of the most important events in the nation's history. In 1803 President Jefferson had purchased Louisiana from a financially desperate Napoleon. Virtually unexplored, the new realm stretched from the

1

Mississippi River to the Rocky Mountains, from the Gulf of Mexico to Canada. Though this acquisition doubled the size of the young nation and committed it to Western growth, Jefferson's goal was not simply real estate. His sharp eye was on the rich beaver trade of the Rocky Mountains and on opening a trade route through the cordillera to the Pacific. In the midst of international rivalry over unsettled territory, Lewis and Clark's feat gave practical confirmation to the President's shrewd deal with the French and validity to United States claims in future disputes with the British over the present states of Washington and Oregon.

Yet Captain Clark had made a mistake. Peering into the rain and mists swirling over the wide Columbia, he only thought he saw the ocean; the real event would come some days later. Given the uncertainties, the slip was not a bad one, no more than a footnote in history. Yet the visual error points to the illusions surrounding Western exploration and the settlement that came after. Hundreds of years before Lewis and Clark, the Greeks imagined a mysterious New World in the Atlantic beyond the Mediterranean, beyond the edges of their Old-World consciousness. Their vision was based on a characteristically human yearning for a better place, but over the centuries the ideal took on a tantalizing reality in the minds of Europeans. From Ireland to Spain adventurers dreamed of rich, if not magical, kingdoms across the sea — St. Brandon, Antillia, El Dorado, the New Jerusalem, the Seven Cities of Cíbola. Where, if they might not perpetuate youth by sipping potent fountains, they might at least enrich themselves with pearls and gold, with furs and fruits of fantastic gardens. The fables were complex, equal to men's greed and ability to deceive themselves. One Mexican historian has commented that Europeans did not discover the New World, they invented it. Columbus, along with the English, French, and Dutch explorers coming after, carried these dreams with him, and hundreds of years later they persisted as misconceptions about the land. When belatedly examined and challenged by more rational and foresighted men and women, they would give birth to the conservation movement, a phenomenon of the American West.

Lewis and Clark, enlightened men hand-picked by Jefferson, shared few of the delusions. Yet when they triumphantly dipped hands and feet into the Pacific, they gave new life to the old fantasies. Their glimpse of a new world revealed new beasts and strange Indians, gloomy forests and unbelievable peaks. What lay out there for the taking, what rich empires existed to be exploited, no one knew for certain. Lewis and Clark's brief look rekindled old myths in the mind of a nation itching for expansion. So their expedition was a beginning, but it also marked an end. Lewis and Clark had reached the Pacific Ocean, the last of the continent, the end of the open road. Though no one bothered to ponder the idea at the time, they had finished what Columbus had begun three hundred years earlier.

The land once lay pristine from ocean to ocean, barely altered by the scattered Indian tribes that for uncounted centuries had warred on each other and drawn sustenance from the earth. Then the European tidal wave spun off by the Industrial Revolution slowly pushed the movable feast of the frontier toward the Mississippi. In the minds of settlers, everything in the treasure house of the receding wilderness existed for their taking. Politics, philosophy, and religion — in addition to the old myths — provided ample justification for their greed. To the pioneers, free, or at least cheap, land formed the very basis of democracy. Emerson, disciple of the "trickle-down" theory of economics, became one of many who extolled the captains of industry, exploiters of the earth whose projects, he believed, created work for those with less enterprising tendencies. And had not God Himself delivered the wild continent as a gift into the hands of the Europeans? Not only was it their economic right and patriotic duty, but their divine obligation to civilize the wilderness with cities and farms, factories and cattle, to use it for what in their eyes was the betterment of the society He smiled on. These views meshed with a pervading nineteenth-century optimism assuring Europeans spreading around the globe that their arts and technology meant progress. Furthermore, especially in America, land and its wealth seemed without end, as riches often do in childhood fantasies. The historian G. Michael McCarthy sums up traditional pioneer attitudes:

> . . . the philosophy of westward-moving pioneers was simple: the land was theirs to do with as they pleased. That their creed often led to land and resource devastation apparently was unimportant to them; raised, as they had been, on the concept of the West as the "Garden of the World," where resources were inexhaustible, they found no difficulty in justifying their actions. . . . Their "mission," as they conceived it, was to spread civilization across the West; if they wasted some of the nation's trust in the process, it mattered little. What mattered was civilization *then*. Future generations could take care of themselves.

With less than half of the present United States brought under control, almost no one thought about the consequences of waste. A few—a very few—did. Presidents George Washington and Thomas Jefferson pondered ways of renewing depleted soils on their estates. John Quincy Adams stormed at government giveaways of public land to speculators. A rare breed of naturalists, among them John James Audubon, tracked through the wilderness, awestruck at nature's variety. Edmund Ruffin, alarmed by his eroding homeland, tried to convert fellow Southerners to contour plowing and crop rotation; in Wis-

consin, Increase Lapham buttonholed new Scottish settlers and asked what they expected to do when their choice
hardwood forests ran out. But few wanted to hear bad
news in a booming land. George Perkins Marsh was a
Vermont lawyer and businessman, later a Congressman
and ambassador, whose interests ranged from discourses
on Icelandic to translations of Goethe. He devoted much of
his mature scholarship to recording man's worldwide
dismantling of his natural home. Yet Marsh's tome, *Man
and Nature* (1864), an early conservation jeremiad, stayed
no logger's arm.

That quaint New England misfit, Thoreau, declared
that a town was saved by its surrounding wildness. When
he observed dam construction on the Concord River, he
alone thought to ask, ". . . who hears the fishes when they
cry?" Yet at his funeral his more famous neighbor, Emerson, honored him by lamenting that "he had no ambition,"
that he had not devoted his rare genius to "engineering for
all America." His footloose friend had wasted his life musing in the woods, "the captain of a huckleberry-party."

In contrast, David Crockett's boast that he'd recently
killed 105 bears satisfied the public that he qualified to sit
in Tennessee's legislature. The small minority that might
question such wisdom was "branded as peculiar or even
undemocratic" according to J. Frank Dobie: "The mass
rule then, as now was: Conform and be dull." Those who
looked upon nature as anything other than a treasure
trove to be sacked were the "stray oddities" of a solidly
utilitarian culture.

And so, as the doors of the West flew open to exploitation, great chunks of the East lay stripped. If loggers had
cut huge swaths from New England to Wisconsin, leaving
economically depressed towns founded on steady timber
supplies, if the game was all but hunted out, and if tobacco
and cotton had sucked the nutrients from much of the
South, it didn't seem to matter. New fields and woodlands

lay westward. Then, too, with its moderate climate and ample rainfall, the East was a forgiving place. With sufficient time, abandoned farm and woodland would restore itself to at least a semblance of former abundance. What would much later become known as conservation didn't take hold in the East simply because there didn't seem to be a need for it.

Meanwhile, the greatest immigration in human history floated across the Atlantic, arriving storm-tossed and bewildered on Ellis Island. Bursting at its geographical seams, by the mid-nineteenth century the nation was launching its wagons across the Mississippi, the pioneers carrying not only expansive dreams of plenty but farming techniques learned in Ohio and Kentucky, in Germany and Sweden.

For a while these methods worked. When first sliced by plows, the dark, wet prairie soils of Iowa and Minnesota responded with the stunning crops from virgin lands that had been storing up their fertility for centuries, inspiring such auspicious place-names as Blooming Prairie, Pleasanton, Spring Valley. The myth of the Garden was confirmed. In addition, the trans-Mississippi West was not settled in a steady and civilizing progression of new farms marching toward the Pacific. Settlers tended to leapfrog the drier plains and the jagged mass of the Rockies beyond, intent on easy gold in California and the temperate valleys of Washington and Oregon. It was only when the migrant wave curled back on itself toward the vast interior and when the old notions of abundance failed there that the nation started to come to terms with the unique realities of the new lands. Then the environmental awareness now widespread in the world began, a phenomenon of the Western United States. And it began because several unique factors came together in the American West and demanded that it begin.

First of all, under the pressures of increasing population

the supply of land eventually ran out, giving the lie to
Jefferson's vision of a democracy founded on the prosperous farmsteads of yeomen. By the 1880's the frontier had
disappeared, and for years before that there had been few
blank spaces on the Western maps, the vacuums that once
absorbed immigrants. Farms filled the most fertile valleys, relegating future homesteaders to marginal land.
Barbed wire fenced off the once free grass of the open
range. Still following their visions, new settlers thought
there was more open land back in the mountains, but
when the hopeful got there, they were likely to find that
others — often aggressive corporate interests — had arrived ahead of them with no-trespassing signs.

Beyond the fact that the nation had reached the geographic end of its open road, that it no longer could escape
the environmental problems it created by leaving them
behind, was another, perhaps more confounding reality.
The West was a far different place than the East, as
Wallace Stegner aptly points out in *Beyond the 100th
Meridian:*

> A mode of life that despite varying soils and a transi-
> tion from woods to prairies had been essentially
> uniform from the east coast through Kentucky and
> Ohio and on to the Missouri or slightly beyond, met in
> the West, increasingly varied topography, climate,
> altitudes, crops, opportunities, problems. The Middle
> West, geographically and socially and economically,
> was simple; the West was complex. Instead of the
> gentle roll of the great valley there were high plains,
> great mountain ranges, alkali valleys, dead lake bot-
> toms, alluvial benchlands. Instead of trees or oak
> openings there were grasslands, badlands, timbered
> mountains, rain forests and rain-shadow deserts,
> climates that ran the scale from Vermont to the Sa-
> hara.

However, he goes on to emphasize, the overriding differ-

ence of the West was not the ghosts of snow-capped peaks
on the pioneers' horizons nor the sea-like plains they spent
weeks crossing, but a single meteorological fact that de-
fied the culture's grand vision: aridity. Dryness is the one
feature setting the West apart from the East. With few
exceptions, beyond the 100th meridian, an imaginary
north-south line running from the Dakotas through central Texas, the land receives less than twenty inches of
moisture a year. In such country, farmers had little hope
of success without cooperation with each other and without the massive irrigation projects that only the government could afford to build. Both ran counter to the attitudes they brought with them, to the laissez-faire spirit
of the nation as a whole.

In short, the way of life learned elsewhere failed to work
in the different circumstances of the West. Cattle died
howling for water, and the cuttings carried carefully
wrapped in wet burlap over hundreds of miles were
blasted to dust when exposed to the dry winds. Farms and
ranches took hold in the more favored places, and cities
rose as newcomers overdrew their accounts with the land
and the water tables underneath it. But the West was a far
more fragile place than the East; stripped of its grass cover
and slow-growing forests, pushed beyond its capacity to
produce, the earth slid into a downward spiral, one that
has continued over the few decades since the frontier, as
current water shortages and spreading erosion bear witness.

The greatest failure — an all-too-human one that persists — is that once having failed to create a stable relationship with the earth, settlers did not change their
ways. Examples of alternatives existed all around them.
For hundreds of years Indians in the Southwest deserts
raised corn by an obsessive stewardship of the scarce
moisture. Without either advanced machinery or much
capital the Mormons of Utah developed a successful farm-

ing society based on cooperation, but their model was ignored by the mass of eager pioneers. The very cactuses and lizards proclaimed the truism that in arid regions conservation, not waste, is the watchword of survival. Only a massive and unlikely conversion of the federal government — indeed of the entire culture — could have saved the West from itself by instituting cautious, cooperative, and reasonable development. But as long as they could sink wells to suck out the last water from aquifers, as long as they could turn their sheep and goats loose on the last feeble grasses of overgrazed ranges, settlers clung to the old ways.

The great irony of the rapid demolition of the West still is lost on many Westerners. Instead of creating an Eden for their children, they destroyed the dream. Suffused with illusions of independence, they skimmed resources, stifling rather than encouraging individualism. Corporations capitalized in the East and in Europe moved in to buy out bankrupt ranches, assembling them into huge agricultural enterprises, using them as tax advantages for absentee owners, dividing them when most profitable into the flimsy suburbs of Phoenix and Missoula. A society priding itself on self-help and self-determination grew to depend increasingly on handouts in the form of farm subsidies and public works from a regulation-entangling central government. Thirty years ago, Utah's Bernard De-Voto lectured fellow Westerners in a *Harper's* article, "The West Against Itself," that their country had become a colony of the East, a province plundering itself for short-term gains, but few wished to admit the unpleasant truth.

Of course, overzealous exploitation didn't take place only in the United States. Armed with technology, nineteenth-century Europeans roamed the continents in search of resources. Often — in Australia, South America, and Africa — they encountered similar factors of aridity and rapidly filling spaces that obtained in the trans-Mississippi West. A few, such as the writer W. H. Hudson, saddened at the plunder, but most accepted the loss in exchange for what they saw as progress, as a necessary way of wresting a livelihood from the land. Nonetheless, English, French, German, and Spanish colonists gave rise to no widespread conservation movement. The present worldwide environmental consciousness has roots as a unique product of the American West. There the whole texture of society's slow and reluctant coming to terms with the new geographical realities inspired a few questioners of the status quo — and, most importantly, made it possible for their insistent voices to be heard, generating a clamor for change. Though, as with other reforms, conservation is entangled in the skein of the culture, it is possible to sort out a few of the individual strands in order to see how, when combined, they produce a slow shifting in values that continues to the present. Some of the factors at first appear to be grossly anti-environmental, but when developed and expanded they had a positive effect.

Pluralistic, growing, its values changing rapidly, the United States was far less rigid than societies with direct ties to European countries. On the one hand, its rather simple belief in the progress of civilization condoned the exploitation of nature. On the other, that very belief, open-ended as it was, demanded foresight as well as introspection on the part of those capable of vision beyond the immediate gains of populating the West with cattle and stripping its mountains of minerals and trees. The nearly sacred concept of democracy inspired millions with the opportunistic notion that everyone — whether Eastern railroad magnate or industrious Irish immigrant — should have an equal crack at nature's riches. However, if it encouraged a "come-and-get-it" frenzy, so that some ranchers seized water holes and hired gunmen to chase away settlers who came too late, it also gave rise to grass-roots demands that the government control monopolies.

Then, too, the land was ravaged quickly, in a few generations, so that in some cases an individual could see the consequences. When Gifford Pinchot faced a hostile audience of cattlemen in the opera house of Cripple Creek, Colorado, to explain the benefits of the country's new forest reserves, many vilified him as more despotic than the Czar of Russia, a traitor to the pioneers, who in their view had tamed wild nature with their sweat and blood. Many ranchers, however, had suffered personally from the destruction of grasslands by uncontrolled grazing and from their usurpation by the powerful few. Evangelistic and undaunted, Pinchot kept coming back to the West to allay fears about his government programs. Some began to recognize the wisdom — and financial benefit to themselves — of a government that would protect the common man, not only against environmental abuses detrimental to his purse, but also against "unfair competition in the use of the range." To Pinchot and President Roosevelt, conservation meant "the general prosperity of the country," and that took long-range planning. And the rights the government was protecting were those of future generations as well. Pinchot's declamation that "forestry is therefore the handmaid of civilization," appealing both to the patriotism and business sense of his audiences, gave a new twist to old beliefs.

Because to a large extent government policies determined uses of the land, from earliest times conservationists have been political reformers. It is a credit to the American political system that, however corrupt and blind it might often be, it has also at times allowed reformers access to political power, the means of change. As concerned citizens, many conservationists — John Muir, Enos Mills, and David Brower — mounted campaigns to influence government decisions from the outside. Others — Gifford Pinchot, Stephen Mather, and Stewart Udall —

successfully worked within the federal structure for more favorable approaches to the environment. Yet the government, subject as it always has been to the powerful voices of exploitive interests, came to conservation more by necessity than by design. Along with the rest of the nation, much of Washington's officialdom shared the myth of the Garden, either preferring to keep hands off the frontier or to impose glib programs, such as the homestead laws, that did not work in the arid West. Yet especially after the Civil War a burgeoning industrialized society required the support of an increasingly powerful government, and the West was so vast that only a centralized effort could make any sense of it. The Army, railroads, mining companies, and the General Land Office all needed maps in order to direct Indian campaigns, plot transportation routes, locate minerals, and document the giveaway of public lands. In response, the federal government, whose business it was to encourage development, found itself sending out survey parties, found itself revising land laws and building irrigation works. If the projects and edicts coming from Washington were more often than not wrongheaded, based on ignorance or greed — often on a combination of both — Congressmen also were susceptible to pressure from those taking a new look at the West.

It was foremost the fact of dryness that forced itself on the government. The West, however verdant it was in the minds of its boosters, was not a duplication of Tennessee or Vermont. Politicians howled at John Wesley Powell's heretical report in 1878 documenting this overriding aspect of the territories under their control. Though Congressmen continued to prefer their dreams to unsettling realities, the situation back in their home districts eventually demanded action as the West deteriorated — as their constituents' farms blew away, their cattle starved, their lumber supplies disappeared. Remedies on scales large enough to be effective — irrigation projects, management of forests and ranges — could come only from the federal government. Furthermore, even those who resisted intervention from Washington began to recognize benefits beyond resource protection. Federal regulations meant payrolls and pork-barrel projects. Though many Westerners griped about federal incursions and stupidities, they welcomed the handouts. By the end of the first three decades of this century, government had become entrenched in the conservation business, and the West had learned to lean heavily on its largesse.

Science allied itself with government. The nineteenth century looked to science, along with the arts, as a civilizing influence. Louis Agassiz and Baron von Humboldt enjoyed public adulation reflecting the optimistic belief among the lyceums dotting even the rude frontier that science simultaneously brought intellectual light and economic prosperity. This attitude spawned a host of amateurs, among them John Wesley Powell and John Muir. The fact that Powell had to scramble to finance his explorations and that Muir never received — and never asked for — the government aid that today, in an age of less faith but far more prosperity, would be, relatively speaking, showered upon them, is beside the point. What they were doing was respected, admired, and listened to, especially back in the Eastern centers of power and political influence. In the late nineteenth century, science and romance had not yet parted ways. One could speak of studying bristlecone pines or trilobites in terms of "improving one's mind" in a manner that might evoke titters today. As far as natural resources were concerned, their development by industry and government depended on technology, and its basis clearly was science. Again in Stegner's words, "Less than twenty years after the Civil War, Washington was one of the great scientific centers of the world. It was so for a multitude of causes, but partly because America had the virgin West for Science to open, and in Washington forged keys to open it with."

For a while, the whole enterprise appeared to backfire in the faces of the eager entrepreneurs. From the growing scientific establishment doling out ever larger funding from Washington, they expected advice on how to hasten their rifling of the West. But what drove early scientists such as Powell was more a fascination for the West than a desire to reveal its economic potential, though that might play a part. Professor Othniel Charles Marsh engaged in an egomaniacal feud with Edward Drinker Cope over the best pickings of *Dryptosaurus* bones, but it was curiosity, not gain, that in the final analysis motivated even competing scientists. And some saw that the elements of nature had unique values in themselves and were better preserved than meddled with by man. Indeed, in their endeavors to discover scientific truths about an uninvestigated land, they often found that the visions of industry's captains were absurd in the light of Western realities. By the time men such as Powell were telling exploiters that most of their dreams were hokum, it was too late: science sat in the nation's capital. Though later years would prove that like everything else dependent on purse strings it could be manipulated, neither science nor its unsettling revelations about the West could be driven out entirely.

The general prosperity and upward mobility of the times were important in the equation that gave birth to conservation. As part of its optimism and faith in science, the country believed in education, not so much as a leveling, but as an uplifting force. And though certainly not within the grasp of all, colleges followed the frontier. John Muir dropped out of the University of Wisconsin, but unlike his social counterparts on the frontiers of Argentina or Australia, at least he could afford the tuition. His academic stint focused his curiosity about nature and provided him with the scientific and philosophical sophistication that years later compelled him into his first public battle and published writing. By the time the nation spilled into the West, its citizens came armed with far more education and financial means than had their ancestors stepping bewildered, and often penniless, onto the wild Eastern shores. In addition, despite the conformity mentioned by Dobie and despite initial misunderstanding of the West, since colonial days some Americans had been ready to experiment with new ways and institutions. Enos Mills arrived in Colorado, a raw farmboy of fourteen. Many settlers around him not only believed in the elevating influence and practical value of new ideas, they could afford to buy the books and newspapers that contained them. Along with other pioneers, Mills looked to Shakespeare, Whitman, Darwin, and Humboldt as essential stimulants. Almost all early conservationists were writers as well as readers, lovers of the written word — as well as individualists raising questions about the status quo— and they were a central part of the intellectual inquisitiveness that helped open the way for change.

Furthermore, the West soon benefited from developments in transportation and communication, often luxuries on other frontiers, though increasingly common and affordable in the United States. As destructive as they were when used to hasten despoliation, they also assisted the new movement with their ease and speed. Mary Austin rode into her new vision of the desert aboard a train. Gifford Pinchot used the facilities of the monopolists he despised to zip back and forth across the West and quell resistance to his conservation programs.

The prosperity of the industrial East provided settlers with a certain hedge on staying alive, providing a longer view of the future. Crops might fail, Indians might rant and rave, but, as was not true in colonial times, safety was not far away. Once society took root in the West, it could afford to think about its relationship to the whole. The nation was knit together in ways it had never been before. The West was settled by people from the East, where there were few natural preserves. True, for years the cut-and-run ethic predominated, but eventually the realization sank into the national consciousness that the West represented the last of nature's treasures, that incalculable and irreplaceable beauty and value were slipping through the country's fingers. As the nation began to admit its past environmental blunders, it also realized, as G. Michael McCarthy puts it, that "If the primeval forest were to be salvaged anywhere, it would have to be in the West." Increasingly concerned about the long term, increasingly stirred by activists, the public both east and west of the Mississippi began to demand not only that its vision of the Rockies and Redwoods be preserved as legacies for their children, but that its very survival be assured through different approaches to the land.

Still, despite the fact that individual hopes for the future have coalesced into lean and aggressive environmental groups supported by volunteer contributions and volunteer efforts, the nation's economic structure remains locked in the old, anachronistic ways. The destruction of nature continues at a pace far greater than its preservation. In his recent book, *The Journey Home,* Edward Abbey tells of Ellen Cotton. For twenty years the widow's Montana ranch of rich rolling grasslands and pine-topped hills has rewarded her with a hard but peaceful livelihood. Now the coal companies, aided by the government, are moving in, offering millions of dollars for agricultural holdings in the area, eager to sacrifice the productive range in one short-lived orgy of strip mining. Though taxes are high and the offers attractive, she cares for the land in a way that corporations and governments cannot understand. Her words sum up the plight of the nation at the end of its open road:

"We cannot keep moving on. No matter what the

price, where could we find another place to go? This is
our home. It's time we stop exploiting the land and
tearing it up. We always used to think it didn't matter, that when you mined out one area, or farmed it
out, or overgrazed it, you could move to new country
beyond the hills, keep moving West. But there are no
new places to go anymore. The land is full. We have to
stay where we are, take care of what we have. There
isn't going to be anything else."

The conservation gains of the past have been significant.
But if we truly care for our children, much, much more
needs to be done if we are to make the changes that will
give them the natural heritage and chance to survive that
they deserve. The following chapters point the way toward
that healing.

*John Wesley Powell in his Smithsonian office. A supreme
politician as well as a renowned explorer, Powell knew how to
consolidate conservation gains, and he had the ear of President
Grant.* U.S. Geological Survey.

Chapter 2

John Wesley Powell and the Rediscovery of the West: Running Rivers and Bureaucracies

> *Remembering that wild look in your eye,*
> *The silent language of your empty sleeve,*
> *And the grand endless canyons of your mind.*
> —Paul H. Oehser

The image of prairie schooners winding on a near sacred mission of westering is deeply embedded in the nation's consciousness. Celebrators of what has become known as the "western experience" less often recognize that during the 1870's and 1880's many wagons also shuffled east, bearing shattered dreams and broken bodies. Some of them displayed the sardonic banner IN GOD WE TRUSTED, IN THE WEST WE BUSTED. In El Dorado the backbone of the Republic had plowed and dug and chopped and stripped the land until visions gave out. Thus many pioneers returned, or perhaps moved on to other Western territories to repeat the process, leaving behind them failed ranches and farms, the spreading wounds of erosion and overgrazing.

19

The attitude that resulted in hardship and abuse of the natural heritage was based on two factors often working in combination: ignorance of conditions in the West, an ignorance encouraged by mindless boosterism, and exploitation of immigrants. Back East, families just off the boat from Europe as well as staid Yankee farmers were galvanized by the myths of riches inflated "by railroads, land swindlers, and racketeers of every conceivable type, corrupt bureaucrats, and unconscionable bankers," as historian John Upton Terrell describes them, who lined their pockets by fleecing the gullible. The newcomers were only too willing, given their late serfdom in Europe or the drudgery of picking stones out of New England's fields, to believe the ravings of such as William Gilpin. Gilpin, himself a pioneer and the first governor of the Colorado Territory, should have known better, but swept up in his vision of the Garden of the West, he testified that beyond the Mississippi "rain follows the plow" — that in fact plowing wasn't necessary, so dedicated were seeds to growing in the Promised Land — that no freezing, no heat, no drought, no cloud burst troubled the agricultural paradise of the West. The immigrants' eyes grew large with the come-ons. Later, of course, they would discover that the land was far from free, that the railroads charged exorbitant prices to ship the corn and wheat they were able to coax from the often reluctant soil.

John Wesley Powell, and others who knew and loved the West for what it was, told the truth, but his advice for more considered approaches to settlement was widely scorned and largely rejected. The *Report on the Lands of the Arid Region,* Powell's 1878 recommendation to Congress after ten years of government-supported exploration of the Rocky Mountains, stands out as a synthesis of a mind that grasped the anthropology, geology, ethnology, and hydrology of an entire region. Just under 200 pages, the volume's forthright, accurate language laid bare the myths and urged rational alternatives to chaotic settlement based on rapine. It is one of the most remarkable and perceptive books in the West's literature, a radical document for its times merely because it told the truth about a misunderstood land. His central message to Congress was simple and yet astonishing to those who desperately wanted to believe, or have others believe, otherwise: forty percent of the nation is arid. Hence, the laissez-faire methods of settlement that worked in the humid East were failing in the water-short territories west of the 100th meridian.

Inspired by wishful thinking and/or avarice, almost every piece of land legislation passed by Congress since the founding of the Republic had benefited the wealthy instead of assisting the yeoman farmers for whom it was supposedly designed. The Homestead Act of 1862, for instance, granted 160 acres to each family. It was an absurdity in most of the West, where a hundred acres or more might be necessary to support a single cow. As a result, large corporations were making a mockery of the land laws. Huge mining, timber and real estate interests, owned by Eastern and European entrepreneurs, moved in to lay claim to millions of acres abandoned by discouraged farmers.

Furthermore, Powell continued, the man who controlled the water effectively controlled an entire watershed. Yet the government's survey system parceled out the land in neat squares that had no regard for water supply. Powell urged Congress to revamp its entire approach to the West. It should grant each rancher at least 2,560 acres and draw boundaries that would give homesteads equitable access to water. Even if this were done, however, irrigation remained vital to farming in all but exceptional places, yet on their own, individuals could not afford the expensive projects. Noting the example of cooperative Mormon farming in Utah, Powell proposed settlement by colonies, which could pool financial and labor resources to achieve what the homesteader could not accomplish on his own.

These mad suggestions piqued the exploiters, who were building mansions in Newport, Rhode Island, with the profits shipped east across the Mississippi — and who controlled state legislatures in the West and Congressmen in Washington. They hid behind the shibboleths of "rugged individualism" and "free enterprise" and hooted, accusing Powell of being everything from a charlatan to a socialist — the same brickbats often hurled at environmentalists today. So bitter was the battle as monopolies fought to preserve their interests that, despite Powell's hard evidence and his long reform career, only now, and very slowly, is the West beginning to accept his wisdom, beginning to undertake the changes proposed a century ago. If instituted then, they would have avoided incalculable suffering, spared the nation such ecological and social disasters as the Dust Bowl of the 1930's — and saved billions of tax dollars now needed to mend past mistakes.

Despite the efforts of enlightened supporters, the reforms Powell proposed weren't accepted during his lifetime. He did succeed, however, in preparing the way by creating a public uproar — and in leaving a significant scientific legacy in several fields — largely because of a river adventure early in his career that caught the public's fancy and clothed him with a certain authority. For this quiet and persistent man, this adventure was a matter of intellectual enrichment, though it might have been a calculated stroke of public relations.

Green River, Wyoming. May 24, 1869. A few men step blinking into the bright morning from the station eating house, where they have stuffed themselves with Ah Chug's canned-apple pie. They troop down to four boats tied below the railroad bridge. Ten men get in and with little ceremony throw off the ropes. As the current pulls

From the perch in his boat on the Colorado River, John Wesley Powell surveyed the lands of the West and contemplated how they best could be used. Skeptics said that he might as well be casting off for Hades. Sweetwater County Museum.

them into the main channel, they wave their hats. On shore the onlookers wave back; some shake their heads. The tiny craft bob around the first bend and are gone. One of America's last great explorations has begun. The odds for success — even of coming out alive — aren't good. Ahead lies one of the few blank spots left on the map of the continent, the untraveled gorges of the Green and Colorado Rivers. Where the only way out is the other end of the Grand Canyon, three states away. Where, they have been told, the canyon walls are so sheer there will be no places to beach their boats. Where they will plunge over waterfalls more furious than Niagara. According to the wisdom of the day, they might well be casting off for Hades.

Worse, John Wesley Powell, the five-foot-six man in the lead boat, already is missing one arm, smashed by a minnie ball in the battle of Shiloh Church. Worse, the expedition is short on equipment. What supplies it has have been begged from a variety of government agencies and private institutions, which have looked on Professor Powell from obscure Illinois Wesleyan University as a crackpot. But worst of all, no one seems to care. In Terrell's words, "No one was willing to spend much time listening to a college professor who wanted to float off, probably to his death, on some Western river."

August 30, 1869, a hundred days later. Four men — an Indian, a Mormon named Asa, and his two sons — are fishing at the confluence of the Virgin and Colorado Rivers. Months earlier John Risdon had caught the public's attention by claiming to be the sole survivor of Powell's abortive adventure. The Governor of Illinois wept as Risdon choked out the story of how he left the group to hunt, only to see the four boats shoot over a mammoth waterfall into a whirlpool. From his vantage point he stood helpless as hundreds of yards below him the maelstrom ground men and boats to bits, while — Risdon always tearfully added — the noble Powell stood at the helm with jaw set, a brave sailor to the last. The morbid account is picked up by newspapers and electrifies the nation, then after a few weeks Powell fades from the headlines. Meanwhile, in Salt Lake City, Brigham Young, perspicacious leader of the Mormon Church, has instructed Asa to look for any "relics" of the party that might come floating out of the lower end of the Grand Canyon. Instead, Asa sees six battered but cheering men rowing toward him. Risdon was a fraud.

Early in the expedition, one man deserted. Just two days before Powell's success, three others, fearing the maws of the last cataracts, left the expedition in an attempt to scale the walls and reach the nearest Mormon village. Unknown to Powell, they lie bloated in the sun, riddled with Shivwit arrows. In addition to the men, Powell is short one boat, the flagship *Emma Dean*, shaken beyond repair in the rapids below the Little Colorado River. But for these misfortunes, the expedition is a total success. Asa sends the Indian trotting off to the little town of St. Thomas, which flashes the news to the world via the Deseret Telegraph. The newspapers go wild. Powell has entered the labyrinths of the Grand Canyon of the Colorado, a thirty-five-year-old unknown, a maimed, self-educated farm boy from the Midwest. He has emerged triumphant over all handicaps — the stereotypic hero of the nineteenth century.

As sensational and scientifically useful as his venture proved to be, the trip was the beginning of a reform campaign, not the end of a career, an early high point that would become symptomatic both of Powell's accomplishments and his personality throughout his next twenty-five years of public service. As even his enemies would later admit, Powell was a gentle, non-competitive man. Typically, when the men deserted his party on the Colorado, he offered words of encouragement and a generous

share of the meager supplies. As a measure of his character, in the years ahead he never accepted military escorts
for his small survey crews, preferring to befriend the Indian tribes he encountered, winning their trust by showing deep respect for their cultures. An instant celebrity
after the Canyon adventure, he carried fame with dignity.
Furthermore, he was a realist. He knew that his planned
studies would depend on further knowledge, and that the
massive amount of information he wanted about the West
— the kind that would support the conclusions of his *Arid
Lands* volume — could be gained only with financial aid
from the government. He shrewdly divided the next ten
years between explorations of the Rocky Mountains and
lobbying forays to Washington, D.C., to support his ven-
tures. He made thirty trips to Arizona, Colorado, Idaho,
Nevada, New Mexico, and Utah, mapping, documenting
the water and mineral resources, recording Indian cultures, sending back crates of plants, animals, and artifacts
to the Smithsonian. He was discovering a country that
most Westerners, viewing their new land through exploiters' eyes, never saw.

His successes made enemies. Other scientists resented
his acclaim. More debilitating, Western Congressmen
representing the banks, railroads, and land speculators
began to look askance at the appropriations for expeditions whose leader went around informing the public that
its Western treasure house was being rifled by special
interests. They began to see the political implications of a
science that refused to obey their commands to speak only
when asked how to extract riches from the frontier as
quickly and as efficiently as possible.

Nevertheless, Powell himself was a supreme politician.
He knew how to consolidate gains. He had the ear of
President Grant, his commanding officer during the Civil
War. Riding the wave of apprehension created by his *Arid
Lands* report of 1878, Powell persuaded Congress to estab-

lish the United States Geological Survey, thus uniting
several independent studies under one agency, a political
stratagem long in the making. Instead of rushing in to
become its new director, however, he engineered the appointment of a brilliant young friend, Clarence King, to
the post. The move allowed Powell to sidestep any political
furor resulting from the birth of the U.S.G.S. It also allowed him to pursue his studies of native cultures as head
of the newly created Bureau of Ethnology, tucked away
beyond the reach of politicians in the Smithsonian Institution.

Within a year King resigned, a victim of the gold mania,
and Powell quite naturally became head of both agencies.
His stature grew over the years as both bureaus issued
voluminous studies recording the West's unique heritage.
William Henry Holmes referred to the Bureau of Ethnology publications as "among the most important contributions to human history ever made by an individual, an
institution, or a state."

Yet Powell never was able to drive the exploiters from
the field. Regrouping in order to protect their monopolistic
practices, they launched attack after attack on Powell by
slashing various appropriation bills. For two decades he
had sat with patience and dignity through similar squabbles, infuriating his adversaries with his candor. Now he
was sixty, and the stump of his amputated arm kept him
in constant pain. Because the later battles focused largely
on Powell as a reform personality, in 1894 he resigned,
thus avoiding further reductions in funds for the studies
he supported. The explorer spent the rest of his life writing
on history, philosophy, and reform, strolling beaches and
poking around in shell heaps left by Indians who had long
disappeared.

John Muir as a young man. The State Historical Society of Wisconsin.

Chapter 3

The Mysteries of the Mountains and Practical Politics: John Muir Fights for His Range of Light

I must explain why it is that at night, in my own house,
Even when no one's asleep, I feel I must whisper.
Thoreau and Wordsworth would call it an act of devotion....
—Reed Whittemore

At sunset in the Sierras some hikers chant John Muir's words: "I am always glad to touch the living rock again and dip my head in high mountain air." To them John Muir is a hero, the high priest of those who escape to the wilderness.

And well he might be. By tradition Americans long for the freedom of wilderness, a wilderness fast disappearing. Muir said that all he needed to flee was to "throw some tea and bread in an old sack and jump over the back fence." How can the schedule-bound and traffic-weary commuter not envy the man who, as Yosemite's cliffs collapsed around him, rushed into the night shouting, "A noble earthquake, a noble earthquake!" At times he seems one of the daring Americans who, we like to imagine, led us

29

West through our short history. We prefer our heroes dressed in a simple guise, but with a vigor and joie de vivre just beyond our ken.

The danger is that Muir tends to become lost in his mythology, some of it of his own making. A closer look shows him a complex man, like others capable of gloom and hesitation. After years of private struggle and doubt, he beat his conflicting practical and mystical bents into an unusually consistent and powerful personality. Yet the most dramatic events of his life are indeed telling, though often not fully appreciated.

One of the most famous of these, a catastrophe that ended in a spiritual change, occurred in 1867. While he adjusted a new belt in an Indianapolis carriage factory, a file flew from his hand, blinding his right eye. Soon after, the other eye went dark as though in sympathetic reaction. For weeks he lay in agony: "My days were terrible beyond what I can tell, and my nights were if possible more terrible. Frightful dreams exhausted and terrified me." Muir was twenty-nine, an age of trial and decision for many prophets.

Up to this time, chances for a lucrative but unsatisfying career as an inventor contended with his love of extended wanderings through the woods. In his blindness he saw an answer: if his eyes healed he would give up tinkering with man's inventions and devote his life to "the study of the inventions of God." As he tossed in his room, slowly his sight returned. Significantly, he described his deliverance in religious terms: "Now had I arisen from the grave. The cup is removed, and I am alive!" From then on he would consistently equate God with light.

Likeable and talented, Muir was asked by his employers Osgood & Smith to stay on. However, a promotion to foreman, a raise, shorter hours, and a future partnership couldn't sway him. Lifting his pack containing a change of underwear and a few favorite books, he was off.

His goal was to walk the thousand miles across the South — no mean feat in the bandit-ridden forests after the Civil War — to the tip of Florida, and from there to hitch a ride by boat to the Amazon. In the words of his biographer, Linnie Wolfe, he was resolved to become "one of God's fools." Yet as dramatic as the file incident might appear, the resulting conversion was neither simple nor complete. The five-month trip provided him with the time and space to mull over conflicts that had troubled him since childhood.

John Muir was born in Dunbar, Scotland, in 1838. Over the years his father's zealousness crossed the blurred line into a religious fanaticism the merchant brought with him when he settled his family in America. Daniel Muir sat in his homestead reading the Bible while his sons labored in the Wisconsin fields. When they returned weary at the end of the day, he beat them for sins they might have committed. To him books, paintings — even an adequate diet — smacked of the Devil. Precocious John, however, discovered that he could do with only a few hours sleep; in the darkness of early morning he'd secretly crawl down into the cellar to read and to whittle a variety of curious clocks.

Though Daniel scowled when he found out about the inventions, neighbors urged his son to exhibit them at the State Agricultural Fair. At the age of twenty-two, suffering his father's parting anger, John shouldered his pack stuffed with strange devices and headed for the state capital. There in the Temple of Art, Madison's citizens marveled at the youth from the backwoods, whose early-rising machine whirred and creaked to propel the reluctant sleeper out of bed.

But Muir found more than local fame in Madison. Like many an aspiring American youth, he strolled with opening eyes among the buildings of the nearby university, envious of the students who had stepped into a larger world of intellectual opportunity. Sometime later he enrolled with money earned from odd jobs, to spend two and a. half pleasant years at the University of Wisconsin. There, after glimpsing the cosmos through his courses, he amused the other students with the devices that clicked and wheezed through their bizarre paces in his room at North Hall.

Restlessness overtook him in the spring of 1863, and he wandered through Canada, then back again into the Midwest. He was by now in his mid-twenties, a late bloomer tinged with guilt that he hadn't done more with his life. Far from being simply an enjoyable interim, however, the time spent in Madison would change and serve him more profoundly than he realized. In the frontier's atmosphere of intellectual democracy, Muir had made friends. His professors ignored the long hair and careless dress of the country boy and offered him confidence in his eccentric development. Dr. Ezra Carr and his wife Jeanne had graciously opened their Madison home and their private library to Muir. On the scientific side, Professor Carr instilled his students with Louis Agassiz's theory that a great Ice Age had carved out much of the northern hemisphere's topography. This grounding in science would result in Muir's first public controversy and his fame in California's Sierras. As for philosophy, both Carr and his wife were self-appointed missionaries of Ralph Waldo Emerson's transcendental ideas. They believed that through the oneness of nature a person could arrive intuitively at spiritual truth, if not ecstasy. It was just what young Muir needed to assuage his guilt and to justify wandering as a spiritual adventure.

And so with his boyhood and Madison as backgrounds, the dropout sat writing in his notebook among the palmettos and sand dunes of Florida's west coast, recording his thoughts and working his philosophical and personal conflicts into a unified view, the basis for future publications.

*One of the conservationist's early and often bizarre inventions.
John Muir whittled this wooden clock and desk to help him study
at the University of Wisconsin. The device thrust new books
before him at regular intervals.* The State Historical Society of
Wisconsin.

Photo by M.E. Diemer

He saw nature as a whole, a unity in flux. Man should stand in nature's temple, witnessing the eternal "morning of creation" occurring all about him. Emerson would have applauded the imagery, yet Muir went beyond the Concord philosopher. Unlike the flights of the cerebral Emerson, Muir's arose from perceptions grounded in science and elemental experiences in nature. Whether collecting specimens or hanging perilously by his fingertips from some yet unclimbed peak, he recognized that "a heart like our own must be beating in every crystal and cell" of the surrounding wilderness. Muir's ability to survive, botanize, and philosophize in the wilds was a rare power.

As his thinking developed, he realized — as Emerson did not — that if nature is a holy place, then civilization, with its sheep, axes, and dynamite, is the infidel, the wrecker in the temple. As Thomas Lyon has pointed out, the view represents a reversal of Muir's boyhood Calvinism. God, not the Devil, is to be found in the wilderness. Nature, not man, is the center of a timeless universe. With this in mind, Muir set his spiritual sights south on the Amazon basin; there he could glory in a nature steaming and writhing in the speeded-up processes of the jungle. But the semitropical winds already had blown him ill. Wracked by malaria, he turned back at Havana, Cuba, in hopes that the Sierra cold would purge his blood. The retreat made all the difference to a beginning conservation movement that as yet had no heroes.

In the early spring of 1868, the former inventor stepped off the boat in San Francisco. All around him that bustling city of commerce — a commerce based largely on resources hauled out of the interior — displayed "the gobble gobble school of economics." In a typical Muir scene, he told of stopping a carpenter to ask the fastest way out of town. Puzzled, the workman inquired where he wanted to go. Muir replied, "Anywhere that is wild." About the time that John Wesley Powell was bounding through the un-

known Grand Canyon in his little boat, Muir was beginning a decade of Sierra exploration.

At first he supported himself by coming down out of the
mountains to work on sheep ranches. The job disgusted
him, and he branded the bleating, overgrazing creatures,
degenerate cousins of the noble bighorns living high in his
range of light, "hooved locusts." Eventually he chose
Yosemite as a home base. Though accessible only by foot
or horse, the striking canyon scenery attracted the more
rugged variety of tourist. Muir took a job operating the
sawmill for one of the two expanding hotels — with the
stipulation that he would work only on wind-downed logs.
On the sunny side of the valley, the sawyer built a little
cabin for himself, complete with a wild fern growing in-
side and a brook running through it. Except for intermit-
tent concessions to working for a few supplies, he was at
peace, free to wander and enjoy the unexplored peaks.

Despite his pleasure in solitude, it should not be supposed that Muir was a cranky malcontent. Though he
could chide people with his Scottish humor, he enjoyed
company; if he had any social fault beyond his slipshod
dress, it was his garrulousness. When in the mood around
a camp fire, Muir could hold forth on the glories of the
surroundings long after foot-weary companions wished
they were in their sleeping bags. Even before he was
stirring up the public in print, with the help of friends he
had become something of a celebrity, something of the
"John of the Mountains" figure that persists to this day.
Professor and Mrs. Carr of Madison days had moved to the
University of California. They sent a stream of vacation-
ing writers and scientists — many of them eminent per-
sonages from the East — knocking on the Hutchings Hotel
door, asking to be shown Yosemite's wonders by the only
authority on them, ragtag John Muir. He more than satisfied tourist expectations of a romantic character of the
Wild West.

John Muir in mid life. State Historical Society of Wisconsin

As he befriended these Eastern visitors, the amateur naturalist made connections that would serve him in future conservation battles. He guided scientific expeditions and showed off the valley to his aging Concord guru. Emerson added the young transcendentalist to his list of "My Men," but he seemed a little taken aback by all the wilderness, so much more wild than his modest Massachusetts woods. Whether intentionally or not, Muir charmed Viscountess Thérèse Yelverton, victim of a scandalous English divorce tangle, who viewed him as a transcendental noble savage. She wanted him to run away with her to Hong Kong, but to his credit he gently turned her aside. However, she continued the romance on a unilateral basis, writing the novel *Zanita,* which featured John Muir as its Pre-Raphaelite hero.

More importantly, in later years he camped out with President Theodore Roosevelt, who happened to be scanning the nation for places to preserve. In his boyish enthusiasm, TR declared that he had a "bully" time with Muir — a man who if pressed would admit that in attempting to scale Mount Whitney he had danced the Highland fling all night to keep from freezing in the -22°cold. Yet California, the bellwether of America, was fast filling with settlers and developers. John Muir's rugged peace could not last long. In one of several striking shifts in his life, he exchanged it for a public career as a writer and for a reputation that holds to this day as the nation's foremost protector of wilderness.

As a late bloomer, John Muir wrote his first article at the age of thirty-four, his first book at fifty-six. Drawing heavily from the journals kept throughout his adult life, he tended to poeticize the facts. Then, too, his mysticism slowed him down; he found his adventures so spiritually satisfying that writing about them gave only a secondary thrill. "Ink cannot tell the glow that lights me at this moment in turning to the mountains," he explained. On the other hand, his beliefs eventually compelled him to write in defense of nature; and, when the writing fire burned in him, he was far more than the reluctant author. A scientific wrangle provided the first spark.

California's State Geologist, Josiah D. Whitney, applied the popular cataclysmic theory of geology to Yosemite. Basically, Whitney maintained that in a dramatic shift of the earth's crust the floor had suddenly fallen out of the valley, creating the present gorge. Schooled in Agassiz's contrary glacial theory and believing in the slow processes of nature espoused by Emerson, Muir viewed Whitney's pronouncement as an affront. By the early 1870's proprietary feelings about the Sierras ran deep in Muir. He, after all, knew his "range of light" far better than any geologist, regardless of his lack of degrees and professional standing. Glaciers grinding over eons had carved out Yosemite, not a super earthquake. As it turned out, Muir happened to be right, though there was at least as much emotion as science on both sides of the debate.

Urged by visiting scientists supporting his minority opinion, he sent off "Yosemite Glaciers." When the New York *Tribune* not only published the article but paid him for the effort, it set the practical side of his Scottish mind to whirling. At the time, journalism offered far more lucrative returns than it does today; writing might be an alternative to his periodic bondage at the sawmill — as well as a vehicle for rebuffing exploiters. Boosted by influential contacts, his articles, both celebrating his country and warning the public of its imminent demise, won the praise and concern of readers of the *Overland Monthly, Harper's,* and the *National Geographic.* Unlike many of the nature writers of the time, Muir grounded his rhapsody in the details of personal experience. He took readers with him from one detailed Sierra adventure to the next. Here he is edging along a cliff face to get a grand view of plunging Yosemite Creek:

> ...the slope beside it looked dangerously smooth and steep, and the swift roaring flood beneath, overhead, and beside me was very nerve-trying. I therefore concluded not to venture farther, but did nevertheless. Tufts of artemisia were growing in clefts of the rock near by, and I filled my mouth with the bitter leaves, hoping they might help to prevent giddiness. Then, with a caution not known in ordinary circumstances, I crept down safely to the little edge, got my heels well planted on it, then shuffled in a horizontal direction twenty or thirty feet until close to the out-

plunging current, which, by the time it had de-
scended thus far, was already white. Here I obtained
a perfectly free view down into the heart of the snowy,
chanting throng of comet-like streamers, into which
the body of the fall soon separates.

It is perhaps a bit difficult for an age sated with television spectacles to appreciate the impact of his revelations,
based on the union of the physical and spiritual. Upon
considering a new Muir manuscript, one editor declared
that he almost felt as if he had found religion. On the
mystical side, the poetry of Muir's words had the ecstatic
ring of a man who was "on the side of the angels and
Thoreau," as Herbert Smith describes him. Muir was having the best of two worlds: new economic freedom allowed
him to garner material for magazines while he enjoyed
trips to Utah, Nevada, and Alaska.

Yet there was a hitch; at the age of forty, "John of the
Mountains" longed for a home life. Again his friends came
into play, this time in match-making. Jeanne Carr introduced Muir to Louie Wanda Strentzel, eligible daughter of
a wealthy medical doctor exiled from Poland. The match
was not as unlikely as it first sounds. Despite his wanderings, Muir could carry himself like a gentleman; by this
time he was a writer of some note; he knew the value of
money and had $1,000 in the bank. It took patience and
subtle urgings on the part of Mrs. Carr, but in the middle
of April, 1880, John Muir married Louie Strentzel. The
groom's literary abilities lapsed into cliché, however,
when he expressed his genuine domestic joy: "I am now
the happiest man in the world!"

For a wedding present, Dr. Strentzel gave his new son-
in-law an orchard and a house in Martinez, across the bay
from San Francisco. Perhaps middle-aged Muir needed a
rest from freezing on mountaintops and eating monk's
fare from a bread bag. Whatever the case, his old farming

instinct asserted itself. With the exception of significant trips to Alaska, in the next few years he stayed fairly close to home, laboring in the vineyards that provided the modest fortune that would support his final and most important years of activism. To his credit, though Muir showed astute business sense, he also was generous with his money, supporting relatives, giving heavily to charity. "We all loved him," said a friend, "for his thoughtfulness for others." And Muir loved the banter and refuge of a comfortable household, one much different from that of his severe childhood.

John Muir's grapevines prospered, but his health and writing, cut off from the strength of the Sierras, suffered. In a way that might not be fashionable today, his wife rearranged her life to deal with the problem. Louie insisted that he spend July through October, the slack season for orchardmen in Contra Costa County, trying to regain his vital contact with the mountains. Though she loved music, when he was laboring in his study, she kept her piano closed. Editors hadn't forgotten Muir; joined by his wife, they connived to get him out into the wilderness and his pen working again.

In time they succeeded in rebaptizing Muir with his old power — redoubled when Robert Underwood Johnson of *Century Magazine* took him on a camping trip to see what unrestrained sheep and lumbermen had done to his beloved Yosemite. The plots of his friends worked just in time; the 1880's and 1890's marked the first cohesion and substantial victories of the early conservation movement. Pen in hand and backed by Johnson, the aging mountain man stood at its forefront. In 1890 the Eastern press reprinted his articles "Treasures of the Yosemite" and "Features of the Proposed Yosemite National Park." Telegrams and letters flooded Congressmen's offices. Saving Muir's old stamping grounds became a cause celebre of national proportions. Congress reacted to the outcry for

government preservation — a novel idea. Forced by popular pressure to ignore commercial interests opposing the
plan, it created Yosemite National Park and provided a
cavalry detachment to patrol the area. Muir and Johnson
took advantage of the public's ire at its loss of scenic places
and of its hope for saving what remained of them. Through
writing and lobbying, in the same year they compelled a
publicity-conscious Congress to add Sequoia and General
Grant to the growing list of National Parks.

Things were going well for conservation. Supported by a
core group of activists, including the young forester Gifford Pinchot in the East, the Enabling Act of 1891 allowed
timberlands to be set aside by executive order. Before he
left office, President Harrison created the forerunners of
the National Forests by designating 13,000,000 acres of
public land as Forest Reserves. Through these years,
editor Johnson continued to be the man behind the somewhat shy John Muir. Individual concerns, however deep,
could be effective in the political maelstrom only through
united effort, Johnson urged. In 1892 Muir gathered a
number of prominent Californians into a San Francisco
law office to incorporate the Sierra Club, an organization
Muir led until his death. One of the earliest citizen groups
of its kind, the Club continues in the tradition of its founder to "explore, enjoy, and preserve" the country's resources. To support the movement, Muir was writing,
writing — *The Mountains of California* (1894), *Our National Parks* (1901), *My First Summer in the Sierra* (1911)
— for a public that looked to the written word as a guide
for its judgments.

Yet in the seesaw of politics, for a time it looked as if the
new Forest Reserve system — if not the new National
Parks — might be lost. Those whose livelihoods depended
on exploiting the natural heritage were quick to call in
political debts and mount an effective counterattack. By
then, however, other magazines followed the example of

Century with strong stands for conservation. And from John Muir's pen came prose with a stentorian thunder that echoed the fire and brimstone of his childhood. Readers opening the August, 1897, issue of the *Atlantic Monthly* found both their religion and patriotism at the stake:

> The forests of America, however slighted by man, must have been a great delight to God; for they were the best he ever planted. The whole continent was a garden, and from the beginning it seemed to be favored above all the other wild parks and gardens of the globe. . . . Everywhere, everywhere over all the blessed continent, there were beauty, and melody, and kindly, wholesome, foodful abundance.

Muir knew his rhetoric. After presenting an historical survey of America's forests, comparing their abuse with the stewardship of Germany, France, and Switzerland, he concluded with a poetic appeal for firm government action:

> Any fool can destroy trees. They cannot run away; and if they could, they would still be destroyed, — chased and hunted down as long as fun or a dollar could be got out of their bark hides. . . . Through all the wonderful, eventful centuries since Christ's time — and long before that — God has cared for these trees, saved them from drought, disease, avalanches, and a thousand straining, leveling tempests and floods; but he cannot save them from fools, — only Uncle Sam can do that.

Only ignorance and greed could challenge Muir's plea. There were successes — passage of the Lacey Antiquities Act of 1906, for example. Its provisions allowed creation of National Monuments by Presidential decree. Because of Muir's urging, Roosevelt set aside Petrified Forest and parts of the Grand Canyon. And Muir, at the age of seventy-four, would fulfill his youthful urge to explore the

Amazon. But in the last years John Muir fought his most significant and agonizing battle — and lost.

In 1913, after years of bitter feuding, Congress voted to dam the Hetch Hetchy Valley, fifteen miles northwest of Yosemite, in order to provide water and power for San Francisco. Like so many plans touted by politicians as cure-alls, Hetch Hetchy proved a miserable, unnecessary boondoggle, a windfall for a few, with the public paying the bills. It hurt Muir that his friend and ally of the past, Forest Service Chief Gifford Pinchot — his eye always on use rather than preservation — joined its loudest promoters. Worse still, the Hetch Hetchy project violated the purpose of a National Park. Muir knew that it was a commercial wedge into an ideal, a wedge that has since been sunk into other parks. In Wolfe's words, Muir "was a prophet of the shape of things to come."

Yet to a reform-minded nation, the lost Hetch Hetchy Valley, whose beauty had once rivaled Yosemite's, became a symbol, part of John Muir's legacy. Stung by its mistake, Congress three years later passed a comprehensive National Parks bill. In 1914 "John of the Mountains" died, but he had shown the way to Aldo Leopold, Enos Mills, and Stephen Mather — and to thousands of others.

Gifford Pinchot. U.S. Department of Agriculture.

Chapter 4

Gifford Pinchot, Aristocrat: Progressive Politics and Despotism Create the National Forests

By far the safer choice
Is to settle down where you are, and try to make a living
Off the land, camping near water, away from shadows.
—David Wagoner

"Forestry is Tree Farming," he said with typical sweep. The idea may seem unimaginative and misguided today, but it was an early step toward saving America's forests from "the most appalling wave of forest destruction in human history."

Gifford Pinchot is best remembered as the first head of the U.S. Forest Service. But he was also a man who for twenty years pined for a dead sweetheart, who thought John Muir demented, who astounded his own Republican party by appointing women and blacks to office, who reminded striking coal miners that though he supported their cause, he wouldn't tolerate their violent tactics. "I mean exactly what I say," he lectured them, and the violence stopped. From one of America's patrician families,

45

he spoke French like a native; he was a teetotaler, twice governor of Pennsylvania, and would-be candidate for President. Stubborn and self-righteous, he was not a man for all seasons, but with Teddy Roosevelt he rode the Progressive wave at the turn of the century. In an age of reform, together they turned their own brand of conservation into official government policy.

The Pinchot family began in this country with the arrival in 1816 of Gifford's grandfather, Cyril, a French soldier who escaped to Pennsylvania from restored Bourbon rule. The dry goods business of Cyril's son prospered, and financial success, together with marriage to a wealthy New York woman, allowed James Pinchot to retire in middle age, a refined country squire, a lover of France, and a believer that decent men belonged to the Republican party. When his first son was born in 1865, he named him after a close family friend, the painter Sanford R. Gifford.

Despite their wealth and conservatism in social matters, the Pinchots shared a decided liberal bent. They brought up Gifford to be a model of a Victorian gentleman, with a highly developed sense of justice for the underdog. He entered Yale in 1885, coddled, idealistic, a little Lord Fauntleroy, but determined for all that to prove his rugged individualism and to find a righteous mission for his life. He played football and conducted daily prayer meetings. Referring to his Spartan habits, classmates spread the rumor that he slept on a wooden pillow; years later his political enemies would characterize him as a snob and a prude. He was in fact a high-minded — and rich — rebel.

Though for centuries and by necessity Europeans had husbanded their limited forest resources, little concern for the future prevailed in the United States. In the vast forests of the land of opportunity, lumbermen practiced only one policy, "cut and run." They skimmed off the cream, leaving behind a waste of scattered slash and eroding hillsides; always ahead were more trees. During the

Civil War, when few were listening, the country's first
ecologist, George Perkins Marsh, warned in *Man and
Nature* that "we are, even now, breaking up the floor and
wainscoting and doors and window frames of our dwell-
ing." By the 1870's and 1880's some Americans were
wringing their hands over the consequences. Concerned
laymen organized the American Forestry Association in
1875, and a year later Congress mandated a study of the
worsening situation. In 1881 it created the Division of
Forestry in the Department of Agriculture, the germ of
the present Forest Service.

Sitting in his imitation French chateau in Milford,
Pennsylvania, James Pinchot joined the first feeble voices
for change and urged his son, who reveled in the outdoors,
to consider forestry as a profession. At the time, however,
there were no schools of forestry in the United States; the
nation had no native-born foresters; there were no jobs for
foresters. When Gifford announced to a friend, "I am going
to be a forester," the classmate puzzled, "What's that?"
"That's why I am going to be a forester," replied the young
Pinchot. The glove was thrown down; he had a cause. And
his patriotic ideas about forestry — that the nation
couldn't survive unless it managed its woodlands for the
long-term common good — would expand to a wider social
philosophy, would make him a trust-busting politician
and an early advocate of civil rights. For the time being,
he had to satisfy himself at Yale with courses in botany,
geology, and mathematics.

When their son graduated in 1889, the indulgent Pinchots financed his trip to Europe. The young man struck
up a friendship with Dr. Detrich Brandis, Germany's authority on silviculture. Concerned about the chaotic state
of forests in the United States, the fatherly Brandis applauded Pinchot's choice of career. More importantly,
Brandis urged him to attend the French Forest School.
Arriving in Nancy, Pinchot was shocked at what he took

to be the libertine habits of students. For a time he considered conducting a personal Christian mission among the
foreigners, but after some thought concluded that the
French were incorrigible. Back in Pennsylvania, his parents must have wondered over letters documenting the
rowdyism of their son's fellow future foresters. Pinchot's
aloofness and zeal to criticize are significant, but in coming years these attitudes would not serve him well in
rough and tumble politics. However, despite the distrac-
tions, Pinchot attacked his studies with typical thoroughness. Brandis advised him to work toward the Ph.D., but
understandably the young man was impatient to put his
new knowledge to work. After thirteen months, Gifford
Pinchot arrived home, in his mid-twenties, America's first
native forester.

The immediate problem was what to do with his training in a country that felt little need for it. He decided to
travel, to get to know the forests he envisioned himself
managing. Luckily, Dr. Bernard Fernow, a German
forester in charge of the Department of Agriculture's
quiescent Forestry Division, invited him on an inspection
tour through Arkansas. The trip thrilled Pinchot, but it
also instilled him with a dislike for Fernow. Despite the
offer of a job, Pinchot decided to have nothing to do with
the Forestry Division as long as the domineering German
ran it.

As to his career, he would have to prove on his own that
scientific management of forests on a sustained-yield
basis would bring greater profit than did unregulated
cutting. The opportunity came in the figure of George W.
Vanderbilt. Urged by the landscape architect Frederick
Law Olmsted, the wealthy capitalist decided to set up a
demonstration forestry project on his Biltmore estate in
Asheville, North Carolina; he asked Pinchot to supervise
it. On Groundhog Day, 1892, forestry began in America.
Pinchot threw himself into the work, mapping the estate,

selecting mature trees for the axe, making room only for the most valuable species. The rough logging crews wondered at the strange procedures, but at the end of the year Pinchot's meticulous bookkeeping showed a profit of $1,220.56.

That wasn't all he had to crow about. His contract with Vanderbilt included an agreement to make a display for the Chicago World's Fair. To accompany the exhibit, Pinchot wrote an account of his activities, *Biltmore Forest*. Flushed with his first success, the young forester mailed the publication to newspapers across the country — a technique he would repeat scores of times with future publicity. In the meantime, he set up an office in New York City and hung out his shingle: Consulting Forester. A poorer man would have starved, but fortunately Gifford Pinchot didn't have to worry about money. Much of the work he did for free, or merely for the expenses involved, but individuals and corporations were beginning to see that Pinchot could tell them how to make their woodlands more profitable. His name was getting around — just when America began to feel strong twinges of concern for its forests.

To the satisfaction of early activists in the American Forestry Association, a rider attached to the Act of March 3, 1891, a revision of public land laws, slipped through Congress. The little-noticed amendment allowed the President to designate forest reserves on public lands. Soon after its passage, Benjamin Harrison set aside 13 million acres in the West, thus creating the country's first national forests. In 1896, when the Secretary of the Interior, Hoke Smith, asked the National Academy of Science for advice about forest reserve management, the Academy appointed Pinchot to its new National Forest Commission. At thirty-one, he was the youngest member of the board; he was also its only trained forester, eager to promote his profession — and his career.

Two years later, with rifle and bedroll he was tramping through the West for the government as a special forest agent, surveying the federal forest reserves created by President Harrison. When the stern Dr. Fernow resigned from the Department of Agriculture's Forestry Division to begin a silviculture program at Cornell University, Pinchot was a natural for the opening. But first he had to pass a civil service examination. Because no one in the bureaucracy knew enough about the subject to make up the test, the applicant wrote a comprehensive set of questions for himself. However, to circumvent this absurdity, President McKinley waived the requirement.

Attesting to Pinchot's vitality— and perhaps his ego — the largest collection of individual papers in the Library of Congress bears his name. It contains letters, pamphlets, and samples from the hundreds of mimeographed propaganda sheets Pinchot used to blitz newspapers throughout his career. Apparently, even in early years, the future head of the Forest Service felt coming importance. His autobiography, *Breaking New Ground* (1947), reflects pride and a sense of mission in his new job as head of the Forestry Division. Yet he was realist enough to recognize the problems. "We had few friends," he comments, then adds, "As yet we were not even important enough to have active enemies."

That is an exaggeration for the sake of humor. The Division had plenty of enemies. They were arrayed in two camps. In the first decade of the century, when Pinchot and fellow activists pushed the word "conservation" into popular use, most who thought at all about the environment thought about trees — and the nation's new Forester had a mania for contemplating trees in terms of perpetual cash flow. On the one hand, settlers, miners, and lumbermen, mostly in the West, where the reserves were, cried socialism whenever the government curbed their exploitation of federal lands — exploitation which the country's

Pinchot in later years, still an avid politician and publicist. While his tree farming ideas may seem unimaginative and misguided today, his creation of the U.S. Forest Service was an early step toward saving America's forests. U.S. Department of Agriculture.

Forester saw as "the murder of our future prosperity." On the other hand, Pinchot despaired at concerned citizens like John Muir. They wanted nature preserved intact as National Parks. To them, foresters were technocrats bent on meddling with God's creation. Seventy-five years later, the differences between preservationists and use-oriented conservationists still trouble the environmental movement. Pinchot, like many today, could understand greed; he couldn't understand the Muirs of the world. *Breaking New Ground* summarizes a stroll in the Grand Canyon with the founder of the Sierra Club: "And when we came across a tarantula he wouldn't let me kill it. He said it had

as much right there as we did." The Forestry Division's
first job, then, carried out with speeches and pamphleteer-
ing, was to convince the public that scientifically managed forests would be in the nation's long-term best interests.

To help his cause, Pinchot organized the Society of
American Foresters, whose influential members gathered
in the bachelor's home to plan the future of conservation
while feeding on gingerbread, baked apples, and milk
served by his mother. In support of its most famous
member, the Pinchot family contributed $150,000 to es-
tablish a forestry school at Yale — a school that would
turn out a steady stream of Forest Service chiefs. In contrast to Fernow's sleepy agency, the Division now sent out
teams to demonstrate the advantages of applying scientific methods to private woodlands. It was a crusade of
bigger and better. With the combination of aroused public
awareness and Pinchot's politicking, the Division was
upgraded to the Bureau of Forestry within the Department of Agriculture. In the meantime, the staff grew from
eleven to 179 by 1901.

One large bone stuck in Pinchot's craw: he had the
foresters but no forests. The federal reserves remained
with the General Land Office of the Department of Interior, an agency with a poor record of public stewardship.
Pushing for transfer to his control, Pinchot plunged into
enemy territory. He lobbied among the sheepmen, the
cattle barons, and the powerful Western Congressmen,
striving to convince them that they would benefit from
management of the federal lands they used. What he said
made a good deal of sense. Much of the West was a chaotic
treasure house just broken open. Feuds were common,
shootings not unusual, as men competed for resources.
Viewing the clouds of dust rising over the eroding Western mountains, the public began to realize that prosperity
could not come without order. Still, though its sympathy

grew, Congress shied from the concept of effective government regulation.

An assassin tipped the scales. On September 14, 1901,
President McKinley died from a gunshot wound at the
Pan-American Exposition in Buffalo, New York. Robust
Theodore Roosevelt assumed the office on the same day —
already a budding folk hero with his derring-do in the
West as a cowboy and his somewhat exaggerated prowess
in the Spanish-American War. Furthermore, the nation
was tired of the ravages of the Gilded Age — its land
grabbers, its blatant pork barrels, its medusal corporations. Even before it read Sinclair Lewis, it was ready for
general reform. Furthermore, Teddy Roosevelt shared
many of the Forester's utilitarian ideas about the need for
conservation and its link with the welfare of the common
man. Before the new President could move his hunting
trophies into the White House, his old friend Pinchot was
on his doorstep talking about the transfer. The President
helped mend the remaining political fences, and Pinchot
gained his victory from Congress in 1905. The Bureau of
Forestry became the U.S. Forest Service, now responsible
for 86 million acres of reserves, renamed National
Forests.

Predictably, Pinchot bent himself to put the new
bureaucratic giant on a sound business footing — thus
establishing the principles which, for better or for worse,
are the legacy of the present Forest Service. He predicated
policies on the vague, if high-sounding, nostrum: "the
greatest good of the greatest number in the long run."
Graziers found themselves regulated as to the size of their
herds eating federal grass; and they had to pay fees for the
privilege. He fought to curb the monopolistic electric industry, greedy for water-power sites. Rangers in the field,
instructed to consider the long-term yield of the forests,
told lumbermen what they could cut — also for a fee — and
how to cut it. Ignoring the fact that forests had thrived for

millennia without assistance from man, the foresters took up Pulaski and McLeod in a holy war against all fires. There were mistakes in applying the new science, and people making a living on the forests grumbled. Pinchot stood his ground; he summed up regulations in a text for rangers — significantly known as the *Use Book* — sometimes called the *What's the Use Book* by the locals. As to the lumber magnates, some of them, such as F. E. Weyerhaeuser, realized who held the cards; they proclaimed themselves conservationists—while hoping for better days and continuing to lobby Congress for less strict regulations.

Whatever the varying views of the new Service in other respects, it was a model of efficiency. Perhaps necessarily, its chief administrator was a benevolent despot. In order to encourage prompt paper shuffling, he once toyed with the idea of nailing desk drawers shut in the Washington office. Dashing around in the field, Pinchot fired corrupt or lackadaisical rangers, while assuring faithful servants that they were engaged in a patriotic crusade.

As has since become obvious, environmental issues need the combined efforts of concerned citizens, bureaucrats, and—foremost—a sympathetic President. Pinchot had the first element in the progressive climate of the early 20th century. As to the second, several important officials championed forestry: James Garfield, son of a former President and Roosevelt's Secretary of Interior; W J McGee,* a geologist who had served under John Wesley Powell; F. H. Newell of the Reclamation Service; and James Wilson, Secretary of Agriculture. Despite their near messianic drive, however, their efforts would have fallen short without Teddy Roosevelt's power and panache. TR had a fatherly liking for his Forestry head and made him a member of his "tennis cabinet" — a collection of advisors who discussed politics while the

---

*No periods. "W J" are not initials but McGee's full first name.

hefty Roosevelt, not an outstanding player, slammed tennis balls at them. For his part, the admiring Pinchot glowed in his status as the "unofficial crown prince" of the Administration. The head of the Forest Service rode, ran, swam, and schemed with the Executive. When Congress bolted at Roosevelt's bluster and growing power — and at the size and number of new National Forests — Pinchot and TR delighted in carving out "midnight forests" — 16 million acres of reserves created before a bill to limit such Presidential power went into effect. Congress stormed; the conservationists chuckled up their sleeves. The relationship between the two men had its side effect, however. As the biographer M. Nelson McGeary puts it, "Pinchot was almost spoiled for any future work under a superior who did not have full and implicit faith in his every move."

Proof of the observation was not long in coming. Taft became President in 1909, and in Pinchot's eyes he couldn't fill TR's shoes. In fact, Taft was a strict constructionist, believing that he shouldn't go beyond the letter of the law for the sake of conservation, even if it were for the public good. The petulant Pinchot, stung and his ire up, picked a fight with Taft's Secretary of the Interior, Richard Ballinger, implying that he was corrupt in dealing with coal leases on Alaskan forest lands. Taft finally lost patience with the head of the Forest Service, who had been tattling about Presidential shortcomings to Roosevelt, off in Africa on safari, and fired him early in 1910. Pinchot saw himself as a martyr to the cause.

Soon after that, Gifford Pinchot's life became almost another story, as his conservation beliefs blossomed into liberal politics. He broke a bachelorhood of forty-nine years to marry a sophisticated and politically active woman. Pinchot applauded while his wife affronted public decorum by running for Congress. Twice he himself campaigned for senator, but twice lost. He did serve two terms as governor of Pennsylvania — where he fought corruption, pushed for social reform, and relieved unemployment during the Depression. Older Pennsylvanians still remember the "Pinchot roads" of his public works projects — the paved roads that made life easier for the state's farmers. He was one of the best governors the state had ever had.

Martin Fausold summarizes the wide contribution of the Forester's later life: "Gifford Pinchot transferred the struggle for scientific conservation of natural resources from a government bureau to the national political scene as a great plan to ameliorate man's condition. Thus, two of the twentieth century's significant tenets of federal government — conservation of natural resources and scientific government planning — became firmly imbedded in the American political tradition." For all that, forestry remained Pinchot's first love, and over the decades, while supporting liberal candidates, he served on conservation commissions and used his considerable political power for conservation reform.

As an aging war horse, however, he was short-tempered and prone to squabbling — he called Harold Ickes, a former friend and Franklin Delano Roosevelt's Secretary of Interior, "the American Hitler" and often alienated potential supporters with similar overstatements. Because of his inability to compromise and a penchant for interpreting disagreement as hostility, he never achieved one lingering dream — to become President on the model of TR. In 1946 Pinchot died at the age of eighty-one, soon after completing *Breaking New Ground,* an enthusiastic record of his forestry career.

As its first head, Gifford Pinchot left an indelible stamp on the Forest Service, which now manages ten percent of the nation's land. Since its founding in 1905, the agency has generated controversy. Environmentalists charge the Service with a long list of specific abuses, though basically the problems revolve around one issue: increasing scarcity. Seventy-five years ago, supporting a population less. than half its present size, the largely rural nation could harvest trees scientifically, with minimum harm to the ecosystem and with no end in sight. In order to satisfy today's enormous demands, however, the Service promotes monoculture on the public's woodlands, sacrificing wilderness, watershed, and wildlife values for production of the most economically valuable trees. Pinchot couldn't envision the day when a society based on waste would outstrip the capabilities of its resources — as is becoming evident not only with trees, but with minerals, oil, even air.

Neither did the agency's first and most progressive head imagine the day when the Forest Service would be accused of falling under the influence of his old enemies in the timber lobby. In *The Forest Killers,* Jack Shepherd sums up the way many critics see the present situation:

> While America became distracted by an economy of excess after World War II, the Forest Service . . . adopted the basic goals and philosophy of the industry it was supposed to police. A few of its officials modeled themselves — and some still do — after Gifford Pinchot, but others became vain and grew less vigilant. Slowly, but perceptively, the Forest Service turned from guardian of our national forests into an arm of the timber industry.

Given his understanding of silviculture, perhaps today Pinchot would realize that his principles, rigidly applied in a different time and under vastly different circumstances, are anachronistic and environmentally destructive. And because to him the good of the country came before profit, it is likely that he would be in the forefront of those urging a holistic approach and belt-tightening as antidotes for diminishing resources.

Stephen Mather with mountain lion club. National Park Service.

Chapter 5

Stephen Mather:
A Borax Millionaire
Rescues the National Parks

I am wrapped in my joyful flesh,
As the grass is wrapped in its clouds of green.
                                    —Robert Bly

One night in 1870 a group of soldiers and civilians sat arguing around a camp fire in the wilds of Montana. The party was returning from an expedition to the fabled mud volcanoes and subterranean fires on the upper Yellowstone River. Now, with the fantasms fresh in their minds, they debated how to exploit the wonders. Cornelius Hedges, one of the leaders, came up with a novel suggestion: why not ask the government to make a public park of the unusual area? It was a radical proposal in a time when any idea of stewardship had a "crackpot ring" to it, when rapid conversion into dollars was the standard approach to the West's seemingly limitless resources. Nevertheless, the men, many of them prominent figures in the Montana Territory, did the unpredictable: they organized a citizens' campaign for preservation. Two years later their efforts succeeded. In 1872 President Grant signed a bill creating Yellowstone, the country's first National Park — the first public preserve of its kind in the world.

It would make the job easier for historians if that happy event had precipitated the orderly creation of the splendid National Park system of today. However, Frank Graham characterizes the age as one that gave serious consideration to making Phineas T. Barnum head of the Smithsonian Institution. To most people the wonders of Yellowstone were curiosities, a national sideshow. In the closing decades of the nineteenth century, Congress did see fit to set aside a number of similar areas, including the Sequoia and Yosemite Parks of today — but only when a local populace grew heady on visions of tourist dollars and was able to outshout the local miners and lumbermen.

For its part, Congress did not envision a coordinated park system, and the parcels it now and then set aside often became refuges more for bandits and poachers than for tourists and game. Each unit struggled along as best it could — without adequate laws, leadership, or money from Washington. The Department of Interior administered most of the park areas, but Agriculture looked after others. Adding to the confusion, a number of units fell under the aegis of the U.S. Army. In the main, soldiers did a creditable job, but their trigger fingers itched. Perhaps they shouldn't be condemned for trying to break their boredom in such God-forsaken places — often hundreds of miles from the nearest railroad — by taking potshots at the bear and elk they encountered. The few tourists who girded their loins and crossed half a continent, only to be greeted by bad food, medieval roads, and shabby accommodations, likely as not returned home appalled at their experience. In short, the parks were a mess.

Then in 1914 occurred a fluke, a bright spot, a memorable vignette in the history of conservation. Franklin K.

Lane, Secretary of Interior, sat brooding over his mail, as usual much of it complaining about his wretched parks. One signature caught his eye, that of Stephen T. Mather, an old friend. Lane shot back a wry note: "If you don't like the way the national parks are being run, come on down to Washington and run them yourself." Mather came, and as fate would have it, he brought precisely the qualities that the languishing parks needed. From a California family with ancestors going back to the fiery New England preacher, Cotton Mather, he arrived in Washington, a figure larger than life — tall, blue-eyed, ally of avant-garde poetry, a man of "colossal popularity" in the business world, an "alloy of drive and amiability."

The new Assistant Secretary of Interior was an outdoor enthusiast, a member of the Sierra Club. Prone to break-downs from overwork, he had often fled to the Western mountains for respite from his business in Chicago. Furthermore, he was not only ambitious, but rich — a windfall indeed for an agency that had trouble luring talent to high-level positions with salaries of $2,750 a year. The cranky magnate "Borax" Smith owed much of his fortune to this advertising executive, who created the famous "20-Mule Team" trade-mark for him. Now Mather ran his own borax company, and at forty-seven, wealthy and restless, he was casting about for some philanthropic cause. He was just the man for the job, and he had his heart and his pocketbook in it.

When Congressmen sleepily shoved aside requests to buy the privately-owned Tioga Road that ran through Yosemite, Mather piqued the consciences of wealthy friends. They pitched in half of the needed $15,500; Mather wrote a personal check for the balance, no mean sum for the times, even for a rich man. When there was no provision in the lean budget to arm the rangers in Yellowstone, Mather bought each man a revolver. Sometimes enthusiasm got the better of him. Waxing rhapsodic be-

Mather in the field. When there was no money in the lean budget to arm the rangers in Yellowstone, Mather used his own funds to buy each man a revolver. National Park Service.

fore a rally in Humboldt County, California, he made a spontaneous contribution of $15,000 to help save the threatened redwoods. Buoyed by the crowd's cheers, he then pledged a like amount from the pocket of his traveling companion, Congressman William Kent, who sat on the platform stunned.

If all this smacks of boosterism, that's exactly what it was. The parks would remain in government limbo until Congress appropriated funds for access, expansion, and attractive facilities. But the politicians wouldn't move until the public visited the reserves in large enough numbers to make a favorable stir in Washington. To break the

vicious circle, Mather brought Robert Sterling Yard to
Washington as the parks' first publicity chief. Because
there was no money for the unheard-of position, Mather
juggled the bookkeeping. Officially, Yard worked for the
Geological Survey, though he was on loan to Mather. The
Princeton graduate received thirty dollars a month from
the government, while Mather made up the rest of Yard's
promised $5,000 salary — more than his own job paid —
out of his private purse. Together they sponsored confer-
ences of leading citizens and produced leaflets celebrating
the parks. They gave gentle twists to the arms of literary
friends, who in a two-year period published a staggering
1,050 articles about the parks. Garnering further publicity and aid, the Assistant Secretary went fly-casting in
Yellowstone with the Crown Prince of Sweden; he encouraged the magnanimity of John D. Rockefeller, Jr., who
helped add needed chunks of territory in Acadia, Jackson
Hole, and Yosemite.

Mather took a boyish delight in his aggressive stump-
ing. The railroads worked closely with him in promoting
Western travel, but in 1925 the Great Northern balked. It
refused to remove a sawmill from Glacier National Park.
Always keen for the dramatic, Mather appeared and invited tourists to a "demonstration." Then in mock dignity
he lit the fuses to dynamite charges planted under the
eyesore. With the wave of the hand, he announced that he
was merely celebrating his daughter's nineteenth birth-
day, which it happened to be. As for politics, Congressmen
found themselves on festive expeditions into mountains
needing their attention. Mather knew how to make them
forget their blisters and aching muscles. A rollicking
camp-fire entertainment might feature a sham confronta-
tion of the Assistant Secretary with a greasy mountain
man armed with a musket. When the official threatened
to arrest him for carrying firearms, "the old scout, in the
process of explaining himself, would slide into a recital of

Yellowstone yarns, lifted for the most part from the buffalo chronicles of Liver-Eatin' Johnson," reports Mather's biographer, Robert Shankland. At a sumptuous Washington dinner, Mather ended a program with a trained myna bird, which concluded its tricks by addressing the assembled Congressmen and Cabinet officers: "What about appropriations?" The audience cheered and got the message.

With this combination of tactics, Mather achieved his first goal within a year — to raise public awareness of National Parks. World War I helped the promotional effort. Cut off from travel to Europe, American tourists followed Mather's propaganda west to the improved park facilities. They came back marvelling at their discoveries; Congress' fingers loosened on the purse strings. However, Stephen Mather, good businessman that he was, always looked ahead. The parks still limped along under the direction of three agencies. Even as his visitor statistics soared and the preserves grew in size and number, he realized that park units must be brought under a single bureau if they were to survive constant pressures for exploitation.

Conservationists had tried to pilot a Parks Bill through Congress in 1912 and 1913. Both times their efforts failed, torpedoed by those who scoffed at the preservation of wildlands as unnecessary. Such powerful government leaders as Gifford Pinchot, Chief of the young Forest Service, wanted nothing to do with the birth of a bureau that would be his rival, that would preserve the forests he wanted to cut down, albeit scientifically. Nevertheless, the climate was changing, and in 1916 Representative Kent of California submitted a Parks Bill. It had been honed and polished by the jinns of the early conservation movement: Mather himself and his assistant Horace Albright; Robert Marshall; the writer Enos Mills; Gilbert Grosvenor, editor of the *National Geographic Magazine*; and the landscape

Stephen Mather. National Park Service.

architect Frederick Law Olmsted, whose father had designed Central Park. They were aided by J. Horace McFarland, whose American Civic Association had kept the drums beating for the parks.

While the bill's chief opponent, Congressman William Stafford, was flailing away on the golf links — where Mather's confederates lured him — the bill passed through the House on a drowsy Friday afternoon in August. Eager to sew up the scheme, Albright dashed over to the White House and convinced the legislative clerk to slip the bill in with others awaiting President Wilson's signature. The Park Service Act became law a few hours later.

Its provisions brought order out of chaos. They placed all federal parks under the control of the National Park Service, a new bureau under the Department of Interior. The organization's purpose was "to conserve the scenery and the natural and historic objects and the wildlife and to provide for the enjoyment of the same in such a manner and by such means as will leave them unimpaired for the enjoyment of future generations." Olmsted had contributed the noble words to the bill, but their contradiction concerning use versus protection would create endless headache for all Directors of the Service.

Nevertheless, as its first Director, Mather had a more immediate problem on his hands. At the turn of the century, the Hetch Hetchy affair had created a precedent for further invasion of the parks. Then in April of 1917 President Wilson dropped the olive branch, and the nation geared up for its first major foreign war. It was just the excuse that the exploiters needed. As would happen to a lesser degree in World War II, they wrapped themselves in the flag and cried that unless the parks were grazed, logged, and mined to support the war effort, the Huns would be hammering at the country's doors with mailed fists. In fact, consisting as they do of less than one percent

of the nation's land (much of it rocky peaks), park resources would have made little difference to the war effort
— except to "a handful of bank balances." Yet phony
patriotism carried the day. Sheep baaed in Yosemite,
miners blasted holes in Yellowstone. Mather did the best
he could to slow the damage; after the Armistice he ordered the exploiters out.

The next five years saw Mather consolidating gains
with one hand, while fighting off new raids with the other.
This time the struggle seemed hopeless. His superior,
Secretary of Interior Franklin Lane, developed a passion
for reclamation. Special interests applauded as the Secretary instructed the Park Service to submit favorable
reports on bills that would place dams and canals — the
paraphernalia of irrigation and hydroelectric projects —
within the parks. Mather stormed: "Is there not some
place in this great nation of ours where lakes can be
preserved in their natural state; where we and all generations to follow us can enjoy the beauty and charm of
mountain waters in the midst of primeval forests?" His
rhetorical question left Lane unmoved. However, just as
Mather was about to resign in disgust, the Secretary quit
to take a job as vice-president of a Baltimore bank.

There was no stronger advocate of park sanctity than
Lane's replacement, John Barton Payne. With President
Wilson's help, the new Secretary persuaded Senators
sponsoring the federal water-power bill of 1920 to exclude
the parks from their schemes — but not without damage.
The amendment safeguarded only those parks already in
existence. Thus the preserves remained vulnerable, and
the way was left open for the Eisenhower
Administration's proposal, some thirty years later, to
build Echo Park Dam in Dinosaur National Monument, a
treasure house of fossils lying across the Utah-Colorado
border. Three decades after Wilson's compromise the dispute would galvanize the conservation movement into its

present fighting shape.

Foreseeing such troubles, Mather made a strong case for absolute preservation in his 1920 report to Congress. He wrote that the parks should be "conserved in a complete state of nature for the use of the whole people and should remain undisturbed in their natural condition for all time." Casting an eye on Pinchot, he added, "In fact, this is the only real distinction between the national parks and national forests."

For all he did to pass on the parks untouched, Mather had blind spots. His first job was to popularize the parks, and in his efforts to entice tourists, he threw the reserves open to America's new plaything, the automobile — not envisioning today's traffic snarls and pollution in the very midst of the nation's most scenic prizes. He believed that parks were for people, but the early Park Service did not foresee the specter of overuse from millions of visitors swarming over its lands, each year placing heavier demands on fragile and limited resources. As for politics, Mather survived three Presidents, Wilson, Harding, and Coolidge — a remarkable record. But he was a trusting man and innocently hobnobbed with Albert B. Fall, Harding's Secretary of Interior. As Representative Kent put it, Fall was a "bright and shining light in the world of crooks," eagerly lining his pockets with kickbacks from leases of government oil lands. The resulting scandal, Teapot Dome, stands second only to Watergate in the nation's exposés of corruption. In contrast, Mather's own financial generosity was an effective and selfless effort for the benefit of the parks. But it also raised cautious eyebrows and placed Horace Albright, his successor of modest means, in a difficult position.

Yet Stephen Mather's extraordinary accomplishments outweigh the peccadillos. Because of his enthusiasm the nation has the most splendid park system in the world. Despite three mental breakdowns from overwork during his fourteen years of service, the Director never quit. He doubled the area under Park Service control, adding seven parks and fifteen monuments to the system. He attracted bright, eager employees, set standards for sometimes shoddy concessionaires, and bought up private holdings within park borders. Under his administration the Park Service won favor with Congress, which took special note when Mather laid plans for establishing parks in the East, where most of the population — and votes — were. His combined tactics crystallized the position of the parks as permanent legacies in the country's natural heritage. Upon Mather's death in 1928, Congressman Louis Cramton summed up his career: "There never will come an end to the good he has done."

Enos Mills on snowshoes. Denver Public Library.

Chapter 6

Enos Mills: Propogandist
of the Rocky Mountains

> *Then should I stare*
> *If I am called a bear,*
> *And it is not the truth?*
> *Unkempt and surly with a sweet tooth*
> *I tilt my muzzle toward the starry hub*
> *Where Queen Callisto guards her cub....*
>   —Robert Graves

Thinking that his pet grizzly bear might enjoy a diversion, the homesteader placed the sixty-pound cub in a rocking chair. At first the puzzled animal sat with a paw on each arm "like a little old man," peering over the sides as his master gave him gentle shoves. Then the cub's face lit up. Catching the swing of it, he rocked himself. But in his delight at the new sensation, the bear made too much of a good thing. In a few moments both cub and rocker pitched over backwards — and the homesteader was dancing on a tabletop as the irate grizzly snapped at his ankles.

Our grandparents chuckled at such tales of wilderness life. Yet the writer, Enos Abijah Mills, had more in mind than entertainment. He wanted to promote and preserve the Rocky Mountains, not as a fearsome domain of frozen peaks and prowling beasts, but as a "safety zone" for civilization, "a friendly wonderland" of nature. If his books do not belong on the shelf beside those of the masters, they offer the modern reader a glimpse into their times, as well as occasional heady passages. For these, and other reasons — his individualism, his homey qualities, his often petty feuds — Enos Mills seems more typically Western, more human, than conservation's luminaries.

Though illness dogged his Kansas boyhood, Mills struck out for the West in 1884 at the age of fourteen. Grace D. Phillips characterizes his thrill before Colorado's ranges: "What kinds of trees grew on the mountains, what animals lived there, and would they be friendly? He was small and frail and alone, and a head of bright curls made him seem the more childlike. People wondered at his industry and his daring." Mills' different sort of wonder would stay fresh for the rest of his life.

The boy built a log cabin in the shadow of Long's Peak, near the Continental Divide. Twenty years earlier, John Wesley Powell had led the first party of white men up the 14,255-foot pinnacle in a cliff-hanging foray. Mills would climb it 250 times in his life, often repeating the trip on the same day simply for the pleasure of it. In fact, the freedom of tramping the length of the Rockies was a sheer joy to him, carrying only a hatchet, some matches, his elkskin sleeping bag, and eating the wanderer's traditional fare of roots and berries. What little money the boy needed came from odd jobs, herding cattle or working in mines. The youth's life, if haphazard, was ideal, filled with the uncomplicated pleasures of scaling unnamed peaks. A chance encounter changed all that.

In 1889 a fire shut down the Anaconda copper mine in Butte, Montana. Temporarily out of work, Mills went off to see the sights in California. While strolling in Golden Gate Park, he struck up a conversation with a stranger thirty years his senior. They traded stories about their adventures in the wilds and talked about the importance of nature to their lives.

The stranger was John Muir, not yet at the peak of his fame but already known for his articles celebrating the Sierras. Nine years earlier, Muir had married into a California fruit-growing family. A shrewd businessman, as well as a profound naturalist, he was making $10,000 a year, a handsome sum for those days. At the time he spoke to Mills, he was more the prosperous country squire than "John of the Mountains." History doesn't record their conversation, but, whatever the realities behind it, the orchardman worked something of a conversion on the aimless youth of twenty. Mills went back to his cabin beneath Long's Peak inspired with a missionary zeal "to join in the crusade to save the wilderness in order that others could experience its joys." The young man wanted to become the John Muir of the Rockies.

He succeeded to a remarkable degree. The public was conjuring even more yodeling cowboys and distressed damsels to color a frontier that had never existed or at best lived only in its imagination. Besides this, Easterners had a genuine curiosity about the lands being developed "out West." Mills began writing for magazines and traveling the popular lecture circuits of the day, a figure who could tell his audiences firsthand what the Rockies were like.

Though self-educated and at first shy, he spoke about life in a log cabin. Urban listeners held their breath as he told of crawling up an exposed ridge through "the rush and boom of the wind" to check his air meter at Granite Pass and of nearly being hurled into space by blasts of 170 miles an hour. But his talks emphasized the gentle aspects of his country, visits of "Mrs. Hairy Woodpecker" and "Mrs. Skunk," creatures that came up to accept a peanut or a raisin from the adventurer's hand. To their surprise, audiences learned that grizzly bears didn't wait in ambush for the mountaineer. Instead they provided hours of entertainment, loving nothing more than to sit on their haunches, as children might, and slide down snowy slopes. Yet society was betraying the trusting animals and the wonderland they inhabited, Mills lectured. The shyness left his voice when he urged audiences to preserve the West's remaining kingdoms of nature, places where people could restore sanity and physical health destroyed by too much civilization.

To a certain degree Mills substituted one romantic vision for another. Yet he was telling about his life as he lived it, and his views on wilderness, for all their appeal to post-Victorian sentiment, came closer to the realities of the West than current myths. In the White House, President Roosevelt and his right-hand man in the Forest Service, Gifford Pinchot, recognized these views as just what their new conservation movement needed to gain wider public support. They invited Mills to travel as a lecturer for the Forest Service, a choice that Pinchot would later rue.

Mills' popularity took him through every state in the Union, to Europe, Mexico, and pioneer Alaska. Still, the Long's Peak area, where one of his cabins stands to this day, remained a home base for adventures. In 1905, early in his public career, Mills subsidized a first book, *The Story of Estes Park*. Unlike most vanity productions, the volume sold well. After that the mountaineer had little trouble finding markets for fifteen additional books about wild America, many of them illustrated with the author's own stunning photographic work. Editors of *American Boy, Outdoor Life,* and *Sunset* found their middle-class subscribers eager for the raconteur's humorous stories about lightning or his account of leaping out of a pine to escape a band of mean and suspicious prospectors. At times in these reminiscences, the author depicts settlers as bestial and niggardly, while the humanoid animals assume the virtues of natural innocence. It irked Mills

Enos Mills in treetop, emulating John Muir. The Coloradan was more a lone wolf than a political animal. If his books do not belong on the shelf beside those of the masters, they offer the modern reader a glimpse into their times, as well as occasional heady passages. Denver Public Library.

that his once pristine Rockies were filling up with aggressive miners, loggers, and cattlemen.

As testy as he might get about the invasion, his books are more celebrations of wilderness than condemnations of society. Like his hero, John Muir, Mills had the cheery fortune of making at least part of his living from writing about what he most enjoyed — tramping from one 14,000-foot peak to the next. The fact that he rode on Muir's wagon is obvious, though certainly not reprehensible. His second book, *Wild Life on The Rockies* (1909), bears a dedication to the Californian. Muir wrote *Our National Parks* in 1901, Mills *Your National Parks* in 1917. If the Coloradan's books depend more on anecdote than on a nearly religious vision, they moved the public nonetheless. "He more than anyone else," testifies Robert Shankland, "was responsible for spreading national-park sentiment around the Rocky Mountains."

Some of his best stories re-create the thrills of winter trekking. During 1902-1905, Mills criss-crossed the Continental Divide, measuring the snowfall for the Colorado Department of Irrigation. Above timberline in biting weather, miles from the nearest human aid, the Snow Observer loses a strategic item, his snow glasses. The inevitable happens, his "lids adhered to the balls and the eyes swelled so that I could not open them." But capable Mills isn't frightened in his wonderland: "...the possibility of a fatal ending never even occurred to me," he tells his readers in *The Adventures of a Nature Guide*.

Down the slope staggers the blind man, plunging his hands into the snow to feel the trees for trail blazes. A massive avalanche bowls him over. Instead of killing him, it brings salvation: he warms his frozen hands on the warm body of a dead mountain sheep, which just a few moments before probably had been watching his progress from a pinnacle. One can only speculate on the metaphysical chases that a Thoreau or an Eiseley would have begun at this point. But for Mills, the telling of it was the all. Perhaps just as well; it wasn't a particularly metaphysical age. And Mills' mass audience wanted adventure, not philosophy. Besides, the homesteader didn't have a metaphysical mind. What he did have was a grasp of nature's relationships decades before coinage of the axiom "Everything is connected to everything else." He expressed simply, but as clearly as any writer of his time, the practical truths that men had ignored for centuries. While the Forest Service scampered busily about the West putting out fires, Mills understood that periodical burning was essential to a healthy and diverse environment. Of the lodgepole pine he observed: "It may be said to cooperate with fires, so closely is its life interrelated with them."

As for wildlife, at that time Aldo Leopold, armed with a rifle and a master of forestry degree from Yale, was threading his horse among the peaks of Arizona and New Mexico. While the young ranger shot wolves and puzzled over starving deer, Mills understood that nature goes haywire when deprived of the predators needed to trim game herds of the old and the sick. He knew what many stockmen and hunters still refuse to believe, that far from fixating on cattle and game, grizzlies "are walking mouse-traps."

The Coloradan advocated what must have seemed a lunatic proposal for this time, restocking the grizzly, America's most feared beast, in areas where it had been exterminated — an idea that is being suggested only now by wildlife managers, albeit timidly. Concerning the bear problem in Yellowstone National Park that has had factions at loggerheads for decades, *The Grizzly: Our Greatest Wild Animal* (1919) offers a typically Millsian dictum: "Eliminate the garbage-piles and cease harassing the bears."

His books served as means to larger ends: support for the new conservation movement and in particular for the preservation of his stamping grounds through creation of Rocky Mountain National Park. By 1909 Mills' finances, helped by book sales, allowed him to work full-time toward his goals. Because of Mills' energy and public influence, Horace Albright, Robert Marshall, and Stephen

Mather welcomed him to the environmentalists' inner circle — a group of idealistic but politically suave movers and shakers based in Washington, D.C. For all his contributions, Mills would give them reason for regrets.

On the surface at least, things went smoothly. The band saw Glacier National Park established in 1910. In 1915 Mills glowed at the dedication of his Rocky Mountain National Park, the august ceremony supervised by none other than Enos A. Mills himself. Riding the wave of successes, the next year he helped frame the bill creating a unified National Park Service.

Yet years of solitude among the peaks of Colorado had shaped Mills' temperament. Despite the gentle qualities of his popular books, he was more a lone wolf than a political animal. He was, to some of his colleagues at least, something of a curmudgeon. According to one of his many allegations, the Forest Service deliberately overgrazed areas in order to degrade the land and thus prevent transfer of its holdings to the rival Park Service. Mills probably had a valid case against the Forest Service — the agency is accused of similar tactics to this day — but the methods that he used to press this charge brought more discord than results. Robert Shankland is ready to give Mills high praise for his accomplishments, though he also places the conservationist in an earthly perspective:

> The two sorest ulcers on his psyche were the Forest Service and his brother Joe. Joe lived a few miles from Enos in Rocky Mountain; both ran inns, made pictures, delivered lectures, and wrote books, though without consultation. A wintry silence lay between them. Enos, the better-known of the two (in fact, a kind of celebrity), loathed the Forest Service possibly even more than he loathed Joe — he viewed it as a towering menace to conservation — and for about five years he presented himself to Mather as an ally, wishing, in the Park Service versus Forest Service

differences, to reinforce the Park Service. When he tried to fan up the interbureau rivalry into something even hotter, however, Mather balked, and all concord finally perished in a dispute over the Rocky Mountain concessions.... The upshot was that Mather found himself down at the far end of the target range with Joe and the Forest Service.

Eventually rebuffed, the father of Rocky Mountain National Park was able to shift back into his guise of serene nature lover. Early in the century, he had built Long's Peak Inn, using "fire-killed" and "beaver-gnawed" logs and "roots of dead trees" to grace the interior. Over the years the public flocked to his guided tours of the surrounding ridges and valleys. Children romped about in special programs designed to wean them away from the evils of lowland movies to the more "pleasurable discipline" of sitting for "hours upon a log by a beaver pond."

Regardless of some puritanical tendencies, Mills was a mainline Rousseauist when it came to education. "Natural phenomena interest and stimulate the mind in a thousand ways," he maintained. Left to its own devices — and a little firm guidance from Mills — children's natural curiosity would carry the day, preached the innkeeper. According to him, the approach worked both mental and physical wonders: not a child who passed through his nature school so much as caught a cold, while the students left its gates "as avaricious for information as a miser is for gold."

In 1922 on a trip East to visit his publisher, a subway collision injured Mills. Kent Dannen comments on his death and his contribution: "A few months later the conservationist who had called the wilderness a safety zone ironically proved his point by dying of injuries received in the city."

Mary Hunter Austin. The Bancroft Library, University of California, Berkeley.

Chapter 7

Mary Hunter Austin
Sees God Under a Walnut Tree

I am obliged to perform in complete darkness
operations of great delicacy
on my self.
> — John Berryman

As the stagecoach struggled through the sand in Red Rock Canyon, a figure stepped out of the midnight shadows. The driver's gun hand went to his hip as the stranger called out, "Ye got anybody on board that can pray out loud? We got a man here's pretty badly hurt." The driver peered into the darkness, suspecting a trick. "I could pray," said the woman next to him on the boot. In a few moments she was kneeling over a wounded man by a camp fire, victim of a shootout among desert travelers. "Repeat after me," she whispered. "Christ Jesus, forgive my sins. . . ." The man mouthed back the words faintly, the last hope of a departing spirit. The pathos of the situation, the gentle heroism of the woman, would have warmed many hearts at the turn of the century.

A few years later the same woman, bedecked with the paraphernalia of a Paiute princess, sat writing in a wickiup built in a tree. She had joined the bohemian crowd of Jack London, Ambrose Bierce, and Lincoln Steffens at their art colony in Carmel, California. Recently estranged from her husband, the author was penning the earliest of thirty books on feminism, conservation, and a mysticism based on "aesthetic patterns in the landscape."

The two scenes may seem opposite, antipodes of a woman in revolt against her prescribed role. To some degree this is true. But if anything characterizes Mary Hunter Austin it is not the disparity of social reprobation, ill health, or the constant searches of her life, but integration, the harmony of earth and man. In her, some of the intuition and mysticism of a John Muir combined with the practical, headstrong qualities of a Gifford Pinchot. As an intellectual woman she was by necessity a rebel. But she did not fill the image of what the media today project as the jet-setting, liberated woman. She preached — and mostly lived — responsibility, whether in matters of sex, social reform, or the beleaguered land.

Mary Hunter Austin was born in 1868 in Carlinville, Illinois. Her father, a lover of books and a former captain in the Union Army, practiced law, but he died when Mary was ten. From then on her mother scrambled to make a living, desperate to maintain the family's respectibility on her husband's small pension. At the time, women were kept as precious possessions of their spouses. When thrown out on their own resources, however, they and their families suffered "the strange indignities offered to widowhood by a society which made out of the wife's economic dependence on her husband a kind of sanctity which was violated by his death; dependence that made widowhood, when it happened, little less than improbity."

Like many former frontier towns, Carlinville was just entering what it considered to be the mainstream of

American culture. Mary grew up in a climate concerned with appearances. She would spend a good part of her life pointing to their falseness. The most modest homes of the time hid the legs of their pianos under chintz ruffles, despite — or perhaps because of — the realities of local bawdy houses. Even in childhood she was different — bright, stubborn, sensitive — a child apart. Often she couldn't distinguish between fact and her imagination. She said she saw things others couldn't and was punished for lying. When she was a girl of five, God appeared to her under a walnut tree — not a very good start for a woman in a rigid society. Whether she did see spirits, have premonitions, and read the future in a crystal ball, as she later claimed, is not crucial. The point is that from her youth she refused to be a docile martyr to prejudices.

These prejudices made life difficult for those unwilling to bend. In later years, when she was campaigning for the innovations of juvenile courts and probation officers, her brother threatened to throw her out of his house unless she stopped talking about causes "injurious to domestic propriety." When the first fruit of her marriage was a retarded child, her mother reacted self-righteously, "I don't know what you've done, daughter, to have such a judgment upon you." Yet she loved her family and for years struggled to keep it together. Actually, there was little else she could do. In the main, the only profession for an unmarried woman, besides teaching, was the street. After Mary graduated from local Blackburn College in 1888, Mrs. Hunter took her to California, where her brother was working in a drugstore. Later, the three filed homestead claims at the southern end of the San Joaquin Valley. With many Americans, they saw the West as their golden hope.

And with many Americans, they discovered that their small ranch was a failure in the arid country. The "first winter rack-boned cattle tottered in the trails and died with their heads toward the stopped watercourses." For the next few years her life might have been modeled after pages from Wallace Stegner's *Angle of Repose*. The family moves about in search of stability. Mary suffers a collapse from malnutrition and emotional strain. She teaches school. In 1891 she marries Stafford Austin, a ne'er-do-well from a wealthy California family. His likable qualities are soon out-stripped by wild schemes of getting rich on an irrigation project in the remote Owens Valley. He ignores his mounting debts, while his wife struggles to keep bread on the table and bill collectors from the door. So far, her life is little different from that of thousands of other pioneer women.

Yet it was during the ill fortune of the California sojourn that the sensitivity toward the land and its people that would make her famous came to the fore. While she crossed the continent with her mother, male passengers in the crowded immigrant car entertained themselves by gawking at female underwear on clotheslines, guessing at polygamous households. Even then Mary was discovering something quite different. As she recounts in her autobiography, *Earth Horizon:* "All that long stretch between Salt Lake and Sacramento Pass, the realization of presence which the desert was ever after to have for her, grew upon her mind; not the warm tingling presence of wooded hills and winding creeks, but something brooding and aloof, charged with a dire indifference, of which she was never for an instant afraid."

In the San Joaquin Valley she listened to the stories of General Edward Fitzgerald Beale, who had known Kit Carson and had carried the first official news of California's gold to Washington. She befriended cowboys and the Basque shepherds, whose flocks ranged across the Sierras. As her neighbors gossiped and her husband grumbled, she dug wild hyacinth roots with the Paiute women — untouchable for whites except for rape. The

Indians repaid her kindness; when Mary's child failed to develop normally, one woman walked for a good part of a day "to bring her dried meadowlarks' tongues, which make the speech nimble and quick." All this — material that later would appear in books that Eastern critics raved over — she was absorbing.

Meanwhile, the young woman faced an uncertain future: her marriage was falling apart, her mother was dying. Yet her confidence grew in an "inherent drive," an inward swelling. The same year that her daughter Ruth was placed in an institution, the *Atlantic Monthly* and *Cosmopolitan,* two of the nation's major publications, bought her stories about the West.

In 1903 Houghton Mifflin published what is her best-loved and perhaps most discerning book about man's relationship to the earth, *The Land of Little Rain.* Writing as a profession for a woman, especially for an estranged woman, was still not considered a completely respectable undertaking, but her friends at Carmel provided the sympathy that she needed to follow "the Voice," as she called it, that now was asserting itself. And the art colony overlooking the Pacific, though certainly a homey place for literary eccentrics, was not as risque as some outsiders liked to believe. Most of the flights were of the spiritual sort. John Muir, as unbacchanalian a character as one might imagine, was a frequent visitor. Mrs. Austin interpreted him through her eyes: "I know something of what went on in Muir....; for him, quite simply, the spirits of the wild were angels, who bore him on their wings through perilous places."

In time, tourists overran Carmel. Briefly, Mary Austin was reunited with her husband. Then began the traveling that plagues many American writers in their search for definitions of themselves and the continent, "shuttling to and fro from east to west of the American scene." In Italy she experienced something bordering on religious ecstasy and a temporary relief from the cancer eating away at her body. In London she met George Bernard Shaw and lectured before the Fabian Society. New York's New Theater produced a play with a Native American theme, *The Arrow Maker*. All the while, from the energy often generated by unsettled living, came books: *Isidro* (1905), a romance of California's missions; *A Woman of Genius* (1912), one of three feminist novels; and later, books on mysticism, poetry, folklore. In the opinion of T. M. Pearce she was "the first truly prominent woman writer from the American West."

In 1924 she moved to Santa Fe, New Mexico, and built a house, Casa Querida (Beloved House). She spent the final decade of her life there, writing ten last books.

Wherever Mary Hunter Austin went, decked out in Navajo jewelry and with a monstrous flowered hat atop her hefty body, she caused a stir. It wasn't only the way she dressed. Her mysticism, her campaigns for social reform, her romanticization of the American Indian, had an appeal to many intellectuals of the day, an appeal that bordered on faddism. Carl Van Doren declared her "of the breed of prophets." From today's perspective the praise seems frantic. Some of her theories, for instance that genuine poetry reflects the rhythms of the natural environment, may have appeal, but often they are out of line with the facts. She loved to drop names: William Butler Yeats, Herbert Hoover, Robert Frost. She dabbled with Mexican revolutionaries.

Was she a poseur? Partly — to the extent that any rebel swings away from the norm in order to confirm a new identity. Kevin Starr offers an explanation: "She had a flair for the theatrical, desiring to bear witness to her values through the drama of her life." Some of her closest friends thought her at times "ridiculous," but they loved her all the same. They recognized that the flamboyance was only the glittering surface of Austin's intellectual

Mary Hunter Austin. The Bancroft Library, University of California, Berkeley.

toughness, genuine warmth, and unique vision.

As a conservationist paralleling Joseph Wood Krutch, she gave part of her time to activism. The Owens Valley lies on the arid eastern slopes of the Sierras. Around 1905 the Bureau of Reclamation joined Los Angeles in a scheme promoted with "lies and misrepresentations" to divert what little water the local ranchers had to the needs of America's prototypic city. With her husband, Mary Austin protested what she saw as a peverting of nature for the sake of urban growth. Gifford Pinchot, utilitarian head of the Division of Forestry, jumped into the foray in support of development. William Mulholland, head of Los Angeles' water department, reflected the attitude of government agencies toward the project by regretting that there weren't enough trees in the Owens Valley to hang the rural population.

As would happen in many future conservation battles, the large monied interests easily won out. T. M. Pearce recounts the early blow to Austin's faith in humans' ability to live in harmony with the earth: "A megalopolis like Los Angeles held no greater promise for human fulfillment... than a fruitful valley where farmers, vineyardists, cowboys, sheepherders, ranchers, prospectors, and miners made a living close to the soil. The rights of small communities matched those of heavy industry and a moving picture colony." Her own words are more bitter: "She was stricken; she was completely shaken out of her place. She knew that the land of Inyo would be desolated, and the cruelty and deception smote her beyond belief." Years later she wrote a stinging account of the sacrifice, *The Ford* (1917). While she was a resident of Santa Fe, the Governor of New Mexico appointed Mary Austin to the Seven States Conference, then considering Boulder (Hoover) Dam. Though the Conference was packed with dam boosters, she argued against the project, calling it a "debacle." Then she quit in disgust at their greed and lack of foresight.

Again, as with Joseph Wood Krutch, her greatest contribution to conservation is her writing, which helped change public attitudes toward the West and lay foundations for the popular environmental concerns of today. Many of her thirty volumes suffer from typical literary flaws. Yet her finest achievements, immediately popular in her time, are the books about the earth, the prose sketches, essays, and folklore found in *The Land of Little Rain* (1903), *The Flock* (1906), *Lost Borders* (1909), *The Land of Journeys' Ending* (1924), and *One-Smoke Stories* (1934). They have little of the improbable plots and strained editorializing that detract from the others. Critics rightly observe that in the books about nature she is at home; her literary form and philosophy are of one harmony. If she had published nothing else, *The Land of Little*

Rain, one of the truly magical books about the West, would be enough.

As with other famous contemplative studies of nature — Thoreau's *Walden* or, in England, Gilbert White's *The Natural History of Selborne* — the work is a loosely structured series of sketches about the writer's familiar ground, a synthesis of mind and landscape. Ironically, the peaceful essays grew out of the most painful years of her life, those spent in the dry Owens Valley near the eastern foothills of California's Sierra Nevada. Probing the natural rhythms around her brought spiritual peace as well as ever widening intellectual and esthetic delight. Henry Smith places her with other strong but minority voices for nature: "She has turned for nourishment to the tradition of Thoreau, Burroughs, Muir — a tradition based on an absorbing love of the American land." However, as is true of the best writing of this tradition, hers was not a facile romanticism of escape; as Austin repeatedly pointed out, the land was harsh, and any breakthroughs to spiritual harmony were hard-won — more difficult in their ways than the lesser ends sought by the recent settlers scrabbling to scratch a living from the land they were disrupting.

Essentially, the book's fourteen essays fall into two groups: the author musing on nature and revealing the lives of those who live in harmony with it. Like Enos Mills, Austin thrives on solitude, enriching herself and her readers as she pauses to lay an ear to the Sierra snow pack and hear the "eternal busyness" of water flowing twenty feet below the drifts. She sits still for hours by a water hole to glimpse rabbits playing in the moonlight — watched in turn by a hungry bobcat. Always the details add to a pattern, one of acceptance and delight in seeing oneself as part of a whole, mystical in its largeness and complexity. Similarly, her human heroes, the outcasts of the frontier, are humble but wise people — "indwellers" of nature she calls them. But despite the harshness of their lots — that of an aging Paiute basket maker or of a Shoshone medicine man accepting execution because he cannot cure an epidemic of measles — their lives touch on a mystery not found in utilitarian cultures. She frequents the camps of the pocket hunter, a desert wanderer satisfied with finding occasional grains of gold to buy a few essentials. He tells her of losing his way in a Sierra blizzard. When darkness came, he had saved himself by sleeping in what he took to be a flock of domestic sheep bedded down in a cedar grove. His wonder on waking and finding himself surrounded by wild bighorn sheep, the shiest of creatures, touches on the sense of mystery found in medieval tales of miracles.

Throughout, her sensitivity leads to the imagery of poetic vision. The mesquite tree provides food and shade to travelers across the arid land and "is God's best thought in all this desertness." At times as sharp-eyed as Emily Dickinson, she sees elf owls, "speckled fluffs of greediness," floating through the desert night in search of lizards and mice. From her understanding of the arid surroundings she knew, though the Bureau of Reclamation and the Seven States Conference would smirk at the sentiment, that "not the law, but the land sets the limit." John Wesley Powell would have applauded the lesson, one that the nation is only beginning to learn. For her, the physical world had its corollary in the psyche. Carl Van Doren sums up her philosophy, which echoes Emerson and Thoreau: ". . . she knew that round every man lies his own desert, separating him from his nearest neighbor. If he will pause long enough, receptive, he may be flooded by a wilderness of thought and feeling in which there is the prospect of wisdom."

The literary establishment back in New York never could decide whether she was "a self-deluded crank or an authentic genius," when elsewhere she described Hopi

Indians dancing to bring fertility to their corn fields —
and not only wrote but, hefty as she was, took part in the
ceremonies. Yet whatever the cluckings of the literati, she
quickly gained a nationwide audience for her ethic of
revelation through care. Again it is ironic that, though
some of her contemporaries laughed, her vision preceded
the widespread and sometimes frantic environmental
concerns of today, as technological society begins to
realize the dangers of exceeding the earth's limits. In
short, Mary Hunter Austin prepared the way for such as
Aldo Leopold, Joseph Wood Krutch, Edward Abbey, and
others who have insisted that the time is well past to
change the nation's exploitive ways. Such writers have
moved the country to see the arid West with more ap-
preciative eyes. They have helped generate the broad-
based sympathy that has supported the successful efforts
of David Brower and Stewart Udall to establish wilderness areas and expand the national parks. On that background of public understanding lies the hope for future
compatibility and cooperation with nature.

Aldo Leopold. Dr. Susan Flader.

Chapter 8

Move Toward Holism: "Thinking Like a Mountain," Aldo Leopold Breaks with the Forest Service

When Daniel Boone goes by, at night,
The phantom deer arise
And all lost, wild America
Is burning in their eyes.

— Stephen Vincent Benet

In one chapter of Jung's *Man and His Symbols,* M.-L. von Franz proposes that an individual is capable of growing through several stages. A person begins with the wholly physical, but he can progress to the romantic, on through the leader, and become the seeker of spiritual truth. To illustrate these four stages, the psychologist mentions Tarzan, Ernest Hemingway, Britain's Lloyd George, and Gandhi. Few people reach the height of a saintly Gandhi, or even of a Lloyd George; instead, most get "stuck" emotionally at one of the earlier levels. Aldo Leopold would have chuckled at such a simple scheme, for he realized that man and the nature in which he lives are far more complex than the neat categories that humans delight in imposing on the world. Nonetheless, the course

93

of Leopold's life and thought — life and thought that helped expand the edge of the early conservation movement — roughly followed von Franz's theory of growth.

In 1909, at the age of twenty-two and fresh from receiving a master of forestry degree from Yale, Aldo Leopold stepped off the train at Springerville, a cow town in what was then the rough-and-tumble Arizona Territory. Headed by zealous Gifford Pinchot, the recently created Forest Service glowed in its heroic age. As a new member of the campaigning agency, Leopold looked forward to his first assignment. Getting into the spirit of his surroundings, he went native. Susan Flader, the foremost writer on Leopold, describes him during his first days on the frontier, ". . . outfitting himself with a horse, saddle, boots, spurs, chaps, ten-gallon hat and all the other accoutrements of the local cow-culture."

This was indeed the frontier that American boys dream of — or at least a remaining shadow of it spilling over into the twentieth century. As the son of a prosperous furniture manufacturer of German descent in Burlington, Iowa, Leopold had hunted ducks along the banks of the Mississippi River; but to him the outdoor thrills of his childhood must have seemed a bourgeois foretaste, a mere preparation for the real thing now before him. The wild White Mountains of the Arizona and New Mexico Territories, with their wolves, grizzlies, and sometimes half-wild men, would be his home for the next fifteen years.

Leopold might have spent his life happily "stuck" in an emotionally immature and romantic stage, chewing tobacco with other Forest Service employees, camping in the ponderosa forests miles from civilization, and killing the hated wolf — in short, being a man among men. He did in fact act this out to a certain degree, revelling in the largeness and ruggedness of the country, but he possessed two traits that raised him above the average: capacity for

perception and ability to change. He knew how to evaluate
the prejudices of his times and how to form his own opinions. Yet, instead of boasting of his growing skills as a
scientist and woodsman, he went the other way. As, unlike the men around him, he began to grasp the complex-
ities of the environment, he became increasingly humble
and dubious of the Anglos' approach to nature.

Curiosity about his new surroundings often drew the
young ranger away from duties assigned by the Forest
Service. The first summer in the White Mountains, green
as he was, he led a survey crew of experienced locals up
and down ridges, mapping and cruising timber. The six
hands grumbled about their boss. When something
caught his eye, he would leave work to scout off by himself.
The Indians, then as now on the bottom rung of the social
ladder in the area, brought the eager Yale-man special
delight as he watched them jerking venison in their
camps. But despite the disgust of his crew and his derelic-
tion of duty, Leopold was learning, beginning to see the
effects of two cultures on the region. For centuries small
bands of Apaches had lived in the White Mountains without significantly damaging the environment. Pushed
back from their wanderings over the surrounding plains,
they held the tangled canyons and high plateaus of the
area as a last stronghold, and by fierce guerrilla warfare
they kept the whites out until the late nineteenth century.
Then, when the Army captured their leader Geronimo in
1886, with a whoop the exploitation, the stripping of the
mountains, the ditching, the overgrazing, began — and
with it the erosion, the depletion of timber and wildlife.
Upon his arrival twenty-five years later, the young
Leopold recognized the problem, while others busied
themselves with making it worse. He knew that if the
process continued, it would leave a wasteland for the sons
of the proud pioneers. Though rapid misuse followed a
similar pattern throughout the West, damage was espe-

cially evident in the arid tail end of the Rockies. Flader describes Leopold's realization of what was happening:

> Reducing the wilderness to possession entailed an incalculable investment of labor, hardship, and sometimes even bloodshed. Hence the community ought to consider whether its methods of conquering the wilderness were efficient methods — whether they produced "a maximum of habitable land for a minimum of effort and suffering." Years of nosing his horse into one washed-out valley after another in the national forests of the Southwest led him to question whether current practices yielded a net gain — whether more land was not lost to erosion than was gained by clearing, fencing, ground-breaking, and irrigating. While one individual was putting a new field under irrigation, another was losing an older field from floods, and a third was causing the floods through misuse of his range.

In his youthful exuberance, all this wasn't immediately clear to the new forest ranger, but he was wise enough and far enough ahead of his times to have inklings that the quality of an ecosystem reflects the quality — and the future — of the people inhabiting it. Hunting always fascinated Leopold, at first with a rifle and later with bow and arrow, and his gradual change of heart about the relationships of wildlife to the environment preceded a wider view of the delicate workings of the biota. Treatment of the wolf started him thinking. Manly heroes require enemies, and in the early days of his career Leopold joined his fellows in the Forest Service in a holy war against the wolves and lions that fed on deer and elk. Yet through all the bloodshed he began to understand that what he, the Forest Service, and the local ranchers were doing was part of a larger mistake. Years later he recalled

Leopold in his romantic stage, 1910. As he evaluated the prejudices of his times, he began to realize that accepted methods of forestry were part of a larger mistake. Dr. Susan Flader.

in *A Sand County Almanac* an epiphany during one of the slaughters:

> In those days we had never heard of passing up a chance to kill a wolf. In a second we were pumping lead into the pack, but with more excitement than accuracy: how to aim a steep downhill shot is always confusing. When our rifles were empty, the old wolf was down, and a pup was dragging a leg into impass-able slide-rocks.

> We reached the old wolf in time to watch a fierce green fire dying in her eyes. I realized then, and have known ever since, that there was something new to me in those eyes — something known only to her and to the mountain. I was young then, and full of trigger-itch; I thought that because fewer wolves

meant more deer, that no wolves would mean hunters' paradise. But after seeing the green fire die, I sensed that neither the wolf nor the mountain agreed with such a view.

From then on Aldo Leopold slowly shifted from the utilitarian Forest Service approach to a holistic view of the environment, a change that took much of a lifetime, until it was refined and assumed a spiritual significance for another generation in the eloquent "Land Ethic" of his posthumous *Sand County Almanac*. Though the shift was so gradual that perhaps even Leopold didn't perceive it, two events symbolize the progression from his thinking of game as a crop to his ultimate realization that man should stand in humility and wonder before the diversity of nature — a diversity that should be restored and preserved rather than manipulated for short-term gains. The first was a national scandal, one that drew into its maelstrom the *Saturday Evening Post*, the writer of romantic Western novels, Zane Grey, and the U.S. Supreme Court: the Kaibab disaster of the 1920's and 1930's. The other was quieter: Leopold's joining in 1935 with Robert Marshall and other conservationists to found the Wilderness Society, an organization dedicated to preserving the variety of nature. However, before he would reach that stage of intellectual and spiritual development, radical for his time, Leopold had a long way to grow.

The elk, deer, and turkey that once teemed in the mountains of Arizona and New Mexico had withered under the habitat destruction and hunting pressure of white settlers. The U.S. Forest Service controlled great tracts across the two states, and to a certain extent the agency condoned or at least winked at the laissez-faire attitudes of the pioneers and their sons. By overgrazing, overcutting, and overhunting they were destroying the land on which they depended. When the zealous conservationist

Gifford Pinchot became the first head of the Service in 1905, he envisioned the correction of just such abuses. Ironically, despite the "esprit de corps, pride, and idealism," as Jack Shepherd typifies the outlook of the young agency, other factors conspired to pervert its best intentions.

For one thing, its leaders didn't comprehend that a growing population could levy demands beyond the capacity of the shrinking forest lands. For another, the Service didn't understand delicate relationships within ecosystems. From the beginning the agency emphasized timber production, not realizing that especially in the fragile Southwest intensive logging could upset an entire biota. And, regardless of their wisdom or lack of it, the new stewards of the country's forests often stood helpless before the political clamor of locals, who tended to scorn regulation of their exploitive habits.

As for wildlife, game management — of which Aldo Leopold would become the father — did not exist as a profession. The animals of the forests received little thought from officials whose main job was cutting trees. Cold statistics reflect the lack of concern: entrusted with enforcing the game laws of Arizona and New Mexico, the forest rangers had not made a single arrest by 1915.

Arriving in the midst of the wildlife crisis, Leopold grasped both the environmental and political aspects, and he launched a personal campaign to do something about them. His success at working in both areas simultaneously shows his perception as a scientist and his skill as a diplomat. He was quick to recognize allies. Despite general apathy, some devoted hunters — many of them from the cities — realized the need for changing old ways. Businessmen saw their clientele of tourists and hunters melting away with the wildlife. Leopold managed to wrangle the job of overseeing game work in the Southwest District, and it is to the credit of the Forest Service that it was flexible enough to give the ambitious ranger his lead. Out of his office soon came a *Game and Fish Handbook,* spurring rangers to their responsibilities in the woods. Taking to the field himself, he explained wildlife conservation to ranchers and to local citizen groups; he founded *The Pine Cone,* bulletin of the New Mexico Game Protective Association. All the while, Leopold was publishing articles in professional journals and urging stricter federal regulations. His views, however, were still utilitarian — he saw game as a crop — and, though progressive for the times, still short-sighted. Along with others, he would discover that sound conservation consisted of more than catching poachers and enforcing bag limits, that the environment would kick back at the egotism of managers.

The early conservation movement emphasized selective preservation. The simplistic thinking ran that if deer and elk were good, then wolves and lions were bad. Denied natural predators, the game population soared. In less than twenty years, for instance, the deer count on the Grand Canyon National Game Preserve of the Kaibab Forest exploded from 4,000 to 30,000. The game-loving public now beheld the spectacle of thousands of animals tottering across the overbrowsed landscape until they dropped of starvation. Yet most people were unable or unwilling to see the cause — so embedded was the sanctity of deer and the prejudice against lions and wolves. At one point the Forest Service issued permits to kill some of the surplus game, but the governor of Arizona, making political hay from public sentiment, arrested the hunters. The novelist Zane Grey hired cowboys to round up the malnourished animals and drive them across the Colorado River to less populated areas, but despite the whoops of horsemen the deer refused to behave like cows. Though the Kaibab lay outside Leopold's district, the problem was endemic to much of the Southwest. Still in the developing stages of his thinking about wildlife, Leopold did not solve

the overpopulation disaster, but the faulty thinking that
caused it moved him to reevaluate his own approaches.
Apparently humans could not orchestrate nature as easily
as does a bandmaster waving his wand over obedient
musicians.

Speaking of predators as necessary to the health of
nature was professionally risky in the 1920's and 1930's —
as it can be in some places today. But by doing so Leopold
showed he was beginning the process of "thinking like a
mountain," as he would later put it — striving to understand the diversity of the earth and its "indivisibility."
The shift involved more than a scientist's appreciation of
nature's complexity. On an everyday basis it meant that
man should become a servant of the earth, rather than its
manipulator. The corollary on the philosophical level was
that by living in harmony with the environment man
could restore harmony with himself. Certainly this was no
new insight, when people such as Rousseau and Muir are
taken into account, but it was a novel stance for a practic-
ing forester and influential bureaucrat.

Leopold's fifteen years in the Southwest brought him
personal satisfaction and a measure of professional success. He married Estella Bergere, daughter of an old
Spanish family, built a house, and began a family of his
own. After official duties, he delighted in exploring, thinking, writing. Starting as a greenhorn ranger fresh from
Yale, in ten years he rose to chief of operations, the second
highest position in the hierarchy that governed the 20
million acres of the Southwestern District. Yet he did
more than initiate conservation reform and open the eyes
of the public and the Forest Service to wildlife problems.
To preserve the rapidly disappearing diversity he saw as
essential to environmental health, in 1924 he persuaded
the Service to set aside one-half million acres of the Gila
National Forest as the country's first wilderness area.
This was a coup for Leopold and a major step for an organi-

zation so concerned with extracting resources that un-
managed lands were anathema to it. More importantly,
the new concept broke ground for the Wilderness Act of
1964 and the nation's present growing wilderness system.

Yet in the midst of success, the chief of operations faced
problems. Then, as now, the Service predicated certain
promotions on transfer. Leopold had moved around within
his district, but after turning down jobs in other areas, he
realized that further advancement would come only if he
were to leave his home in the Southwest. In addition,
along with earning a national reputation as an environmentalist, his activism had generated a certain amount of
strain in his district. In the same year as his wilderness
victory on the Gila, he accepted a new position in Madison,
Wisconsin, becoming associate director of the Forest Service research unit, the U.S. Forest Products Laboratory.
Nearly twenty-five years of public service, study, and
publication lay before him, but the course already was set;
his mature thinking would be an expansion of ideas
formed during his years in the abused Apache country at
the southern tip of the Rocky Mountains.

He took his new job with the understanding that he
would soon replace the current head. Contrary to expectations, however, the director stayed on, and Leopold chafed
through four years of administrative paper-shuffling. As a
result the Forest Service lost perhaps its most original
thinker when he quit in 1928. For the next few years he
conducted game surveys in the Midwest for the Sporting
Arms and Ammunition Manufacturers Institute and assisted universities in developing wildlife programs. He
implemented his environmental philosophy by encouraging habitat restoration of lands that settlers had wrung of
their resources, then abandoned. Much of the latter work
brought pleasure, especially his mending of acres around
the family's weekend shack — the inspiration for *A Sand
County Almanac.*

Widespread professional acclaim followed in 1933 with publication of *Game Management*. In it Leopold still showed himself a technocrat, believing that the environment should be manipulated, albeit with greater sensitivity than in the past. He was increasing his knowledge of the environment, which eventually brought him closer to the worshipper of nature, John Muir, than to its exploiter, Gifford Pinchot. At any rate, the text established him as the "father" of a new science. He wrote it in the depths of the Depression, jobless and worrying about feeding a wife and five children. In the same year as its publication, however, the University of Wisconsin sweetened the book's success by creating a chair of game management especially for Aldo Leopold. He kept the job until his death, working with graduate students, establishing cooperative programs, always writing.

Though the shift to the last major development in Leopold's thought is difficult to pin down, when he helped found the Wilderness Society in 1935 his thinking took a direction that would result in the capstone of his career. Ironically, the manuscript of *A Sand County Almanac*, the book that would make his name famous, circulated for seven years, suffering repeated rejections by publishers. Editors felt that the rambling philosophy of the essays was not what the public wanted. With typical grit, Leopold kept revising and sending out the manuscript. On April 14, 1948, an editor at Oxford University Press called to say that his firm would be happy to print the book. Seven days later the Leopold family spotted smoke across the swamp near its country shack. A veteran of fire, Leopold armed the family with buckets and brooms and led it to a neighbor's burning field. Soon after, he fell on the fire line, dead of a heart attack at the age of sixty-one.

Bernard DeVoto in the classroom. The Stanford University Libraries.

Chapter 9

Bernard DeVoto:
On the Barricades

I walked the streets where I was born and grew,
And all the streets were new.
                    —Donald Hall

At the age of twenty-three he sulked in home-town
Ogden, Utah, convinced he was a failure. True, Bernard
DeVoto had served as a lieutenant in the Army during
World War I. He had graduated from Harvard. Years later
he would be one of the state's most famous sons, but in his
youth he wanted something romantic for a career. He
wanted to be a novelist. Unsure of his talents and uncertain of how to accomplish literary fame, he returned home
after college to stew "in his own lethargy and Ogden's
torpor," as Wallace Stegner describes the young DeVoto.
He had watched his mother die; migraines, insomnia, and
listlessness plagued him. The writing wouldn't come.
Sometimes, sweating, full of doubts, he couldn't face the
task of crossing a street. Finally, in a painful effort to

105

break the ennui, the young man boarded the Overland Limited in the fall of 1922 for a teaching job at Northwestern. Gloom dogged him as the train headed east into the Wasatch Mountains past his grandfather's farm. As it gathered speed across the bleak Wyoming Plateau, he felt he would never leave the car alive. Yet he did reach Northwestern. If depression followed this son of a Mormon mother and an apostate Italian Catholic, it was a mood he eventually harnessed to drive his creativity and become one of the most controversial writers, one of the most effective conservationists, of the mid-century.

And if at times the young instructor of English had to wrap his feet around the legs of his chair to keep from running in a cold sweat from the classroom, the students didn't notice. As hard as he was on them, they liked him, so much so that the administration held him suspect for his popularity. He married the prettiest girl in his freshman English class and, envied by colleagues, began publishing articles on Western history. A first novel, *The Crooked Mile,* set a future pattern by capitalizing on his love-hate relationship with the West, as symbolized by Ogden, called Windsor in the book. However, despite his growing security at Northwestern, DeVoto longed for his alma mater, which offered not only the research materials he would need for anticipated studies on Western history, but also the genteel academic poses to alternately polish and tweak. With little more than faith that he could support himself with writing, DeVoto moved to Cambridge. By the mid-1930's the results, especially *Mark Twain's America,* gained him recognition as an authority on literature and Western history. Yet, though he maintained a home in Cambridge almost continuously until his death in 1955, to its own loss Harvard shied from granting him full status on the faculty. He lacked the academic credentials of a bona fide scholar. Viewing DeVoto through its own reserve, the Cambridge community tended to look on him as a "professional Western Wild Man..., the illegitimate offspring of H. L. Mencken and Annie Oakley," as Stegner puts their reaction. Perhaps more importantly, President James Bryant Conant judged the production of short stories, mediocre novels, and broadsides against the ills, illusions, and corruptions of society — including those of the literati — as not quite in form. Admittedly, much of DeVoto's output was hackwork, but it was work that he could do well — he bragged that he could sell anything he wrote — and it brought the regular income that his more serious writing could not provide.

Be that as it may, the serious writing, *The Year of Decision: 1846* (1943), *Across the Wide Missouri* (1947), and *The Course of Empire* (1952), brought the Ogden-Cambridge author the Pulitzer and Bancroft Prizes and a National Book Award. Their popularity and acclaim by scholars helped establish history of the American West as a permanent study in the curriculum of the nation's universities. The books went beyond authoritative research. Rather than presenting narratives in the usual method, chronologically, they dealt with parallel events, weaving the stories into valid synergisms of history. They presented Western characters — Jim Bridger, Joe Meek, Sir William Stewart — in the round, fleshed out, full of energy, raw visions, and foibles. DeVoto had learned much from writing mediocre novels.

Though after 1927 Cambridge became the writer's adopted home, the great bulk of his work, whether written for money or love, continued to focus on the West. Unlike some authors, he didn't tolerate Westerners' delusions about themselves — their rugged individualism, their romantic cowboy culture learned from movie screens, their boosterism. The expatriate son was a stickler for using facts as the underpinnings of judgments. He was quick to sympathize with the rawboned pioneers, to praise the clear skies over the Rockies and the enormous natural potential of the plains. However, he was just as ready to remind his countrymen that, like most frontiers, the West encouraged conformity, that more often than not its rugged individualists had ended their lives swinging from vigilante ropes — that cowboy hats imitated a pattern originally used by Yankee swineherds. Most Utahans couldn't, and still can't, find it in their hearts to forgive the state's most celebrated writer for wounding their pride with the truth. So he sat like a rejected lover, looking back on the West through New England's elms and the superb collection of material in Harvard's Widener Library. With the objectivity that can come with distance, he probed the phenomenon of the frontier, trying to explain its role in the nation's development, perhaps as much to himself as to his readers.

His love of the West made him one of its most severe critics and avid conservationists — to him activism was a healthy side of patriotism. He began writing the "Easy Chair" column for *Harper's* in 1935. From this monthly forum, he informed the public among other things that while it drowsed, special interests were busy stripping, overgrazing, and clearcutting the West's birthright, the natural heritage of America. It was an economics of liquidation. Westerners welcomed industry, but they were gulled by Eastern capital, selling their land short in the same boom-and-bust pattern that had dominated the region since the fur trade brought the beaver close to extinction in the 1830's. The new massive assault for quick gains would be the last boom, ending in a permanent bust. A trip he took with his wife, Avis, after World War II brought DeVoto's anger to a white heat. As Wallace Stegner says, "When he finally came West in person, he came like Lancelot."

What shocked him was the same postwar process that continues to the present, the building of needless dams, the ruin of watersheds by overgrazing. In particular, he

Bernard DeVoto. The Stanford University Libraries.

caught wind from Chet Olsen, a friend in the U.S. Forest Service, of a conspiracy on the part of large grazing interests to twist public lands away from the government by Congressional action. According to the scenario, the public lands would be turned over to the states and eventually sold cheap to the stockmen for as low as ten cents an acre. At such prices they could afford to abuse the ranges as they wished for quick profits, then abandon them, eroding and worthless, to future generations. As a Westerner, DeVoto sympathized with the problems of small ranchers, but he recognized that the plan touted for their benefit would mean their ruin.

He was a man who waited for his shots and, when the time was right, leaped out with both barrels blazing. After his rage cooled a bit and he could complete the proper research, he came from the bushes blasting away at the

exploiters with "The West Against Itself," a classic statement of the West's schizophrenia in the January 1947
issue of *Harper's*. He documented Western Congressmen's
scheme to turn the public's resources over the businesses
they represented. And he chided the average citizen for
being duped by the banner of states' rights held by those
"hellbent on destroying the West." The stockmen and
politicians who were already counting easy profits from
the plan reeled back in disarray at the accuracy of his
attack and the resulting outcry across the nation.

Though conservation won out on the immediate issue,
the profiteers had money and public relations men plus
Congressional influence in proportion to both. Timber,
stock, and mining corporations pooled their energy for a
prolonged battle. Year after year they came back to Congress with an array of bills in an attempt to emasculate
the Forest Service and Bureau of Land Management, to
chip away at the National Parks in order to liquidate the
natural legacy for their own short-term gains. At the time,
environmental organizations consisted of a few thousand
citizens ineffectively scattered across the country. They
braced themselves for the slaughter. However, fighting on
the side of the underdog made DeVoto frisky, if not exub-
erant. Though running low on money to support his family, he laid aside regular writing projects to organize an
information network of columnists, politicians, and
naturalists, most of them old friends. He accepted an appointment to the Advisory Board for National Parks. Most
importantly, he had the broad audience that environmentalists, with their local mimeographed broadsides, lacked.
For decades the public had read and trusted DeVoto. Now
from the leading opinion-makers of the day, from the
Saturday Evening Post, Reader's Digest, Colliers, Fortune,
he revealed the stratagems that the plunderers were trying to keep out of the news. In a burst of enthusiasm
Oregon's Senator Neuberger called him the most effective

conservationist of the century. Arthur M. Schlesinger, Jr. credited him with single-handedly saving the government's reserve systems.

Because of his success, the landgrabbers tried to silence DeVoto by pressuring the magazines into refusing his articles. This card is a powerful one to use against a writer, but it was the wrong one to try on Bernard DeVoto. He had clout with editors by virtue of the reputation he brought to their publications. He informed them that he wouldn't back off, putting them in mind of their responsibility to the public. "You didn't," he lectured them, "mount the barricades until noon and then go out for a three-hour lunch." He stayed on the barricades until his death, writing forty articles prodding Congressmen to react to their good consciences, while pointing out that he was reminding the public of election time if they didn't. When he died in November, 1955, conservation lost a powerful voice. No writer has quite replaced it. The following spring Chet Olsen flew along the Idaho-Montana border; the old Forest Service friend scattered DeVoto's ashes over the Bitterroot Mountains near Lolo Pass, where Lewis and Clark broke through the cordillera to the Pacific.

Margaret and Olaus Murie at their home in Moose, Wyoming.
Margaret Murie.

Chapter 10

Science and Sympathy: Olaus Murie and the Fight for Wildlife

Still leaning toward the last place the sun was.
— Theodore Roethke

Perhaps no country in history altered its environment as quickly as did the United States in the first dozen or so decades of its existence. Cheap land, new technologies, and a swelling population — the very factors that gave the new nation muscle — also tended to leave the land a shambles, its wild species extinct or pushed into remnant populations. By 1885 Yellowstone National Park sheltered the only buffalo herd of any size, reduced to 400 individuals from the estimated sixty million that once grazed from the Appalachians to the Pacific. Though a contingent of the U.S. Cavalry tried to protect them, the species dwindled as scarcity made its destruction more profitable. Poachers sold the shaggy heads for $500 in Billings and Helena.

113

For generations migrating passenger pigeons caused trees to collapse, so great were their numbers. In 1914, Martha, the last of her kind, died ignobly in the Cincinnati Zoo. Similar if less dramatic fates awaited the white-tailed deer, bear, elk, moose, prairie chicken, and other animals that meat packers had shipped east by the carload. Whether in New Hampshire or Colorado, pot and market hunters stepped into the emptied woods and wondered where their free supply of protein had gone. They ignored the obviousness of habitat destruction and the self-implicating fact of the world's greatest animal slaughter. Instead they took the human way: they blamed coyotes, foxes, eagles — whatever was at hand. Equally eager for handy villains, the government launched poisoning programs aimed at the few predators left on the eroded and clear-cut lands of the public domain. A twisted concept of democracy, that each man was free to exploit resources as he saw fit, had combined with ignorance to decimate the nation's game in one enthusiastic burst.

The United States was not alone. According to their abilities, other developing countries of the New World joined in the free-for-all on the environment. Yet it is ironic that the nation most efficient in destruction also led in research and reform.

The colonists had brought the concept of hunting regulation from Europe. By 1880 all the states in existence had restrictions of one sort or another, but enforcement was spotty, and the laws did not face the real problems behind the decline of game, over-hunting and loss of habitat. What had worked in Europe, where few but the wealthy pursued large game, and these on well-regulated reserves, was failing in a land of free enterprise versus nature. In the midst of the rout, Thomas Jefferson, Audubon, and later Ernest Thompson Seton, William Hornaday, and George Bird Grinnell, represented a naturalists' counter-culture. They studied flora and fauna, frequently out of sheer fascination — eccentrics indeed in a land thriving on exploitation. Such men as John Wesley Powell kept prodding Congress for needed scientific support, and when the government embraced knowledge in the closing years of the nineteenth century, a new era began. Professional botanists, foresters, and mammalogists now found places in a government that was creating the forerunners of the Park Service, the Forest Service, and the Fish and Wildlife Service. With the other hand, however, it continued to give away the public's land, nod at the clearcutting of forests, and poison innocent foxes. With the rest of the country, the government shared a double standard toward the natural heritage. But gaining a foothold, a few men were revealing to an increasingly educated and sympathetic public the subtleties involved, that the passenger pigeon didn't simply fly away into oblivion. And though their interests extended far beyond game species, they began to receive acclaim for their wildlife studies from hunters, especially city hunters, and from arms manufacturers, who saw their profits disappearing with the animals.

In the ranks of the scientific bureaucracy that coalesced in the first decades of the century, Olaus Murie is at once typical and outstanding. Like many ambitious boys, he worked his way through school to obtain the necessary credential, a degree in science. Then followed field trips, years of government service, publishing. However, it wasn't only that he became an expert in several areas that distinguished him from other colleagues — though that certainly helped. His scientific expertise gave his voice authority in a society that dotes on the specialist; however, it was more the voice itself, the warmth and vision of the personality behind it. Looking back on the biologist's life, his wife shares the frustration that other writers have felt in trying to capture the spiritual ingredients, the charismatic qualities that moved Murie's followers. She concludes, "He believed that even with the very worst forecast possible for the future, it was more fun to take part in the battle for what you believed in than just to stand on the sidelines wringing your hands.... With all the work, he obviously had such joy in living that perhaps they could feel the battle was worth taking part in. If they knew him longer, they surely sensed that under the continuous gentleness and lack of frustration under pressures, there was the steel of belief, of unshakable confidence...."

His government career reflects his buoyancy. It was not a series of plodding steps up the bureaucratic ladder. In the youth of our grandparents, there were still blank spots on the maps of Canada and Alaska, species that had not been studied in depth, Eskimos who had not seen a white face. His career contained the stuff of adventure that kept the readers of Jack London on the edges of their chairs, though for his part the young biologist emphasized the thrills of everyday nature rather than of danger. Furthermore, Murie had the luck to explore and investigate independently in a way that perhaps is not possible today. Once, tired of driving a dogteam for hours, only to spend the evening filling out meaningless forms about his activities, he informed his superiors that they'd have to be satisfied with one report a month. They nodded and let him have his lead — a phenomenon hard to imagine in the age of the computer.

A close family life and wild countryside offered compensations for his financially poor and strenuous boyhood. Less than ten years after arriving from Norway, Murie's father died, leaving his immigrant wife with a house, one cow, and three young sons. The boys pitched in, selling milk, picking potatoes, plowing for local farmers. With his brother Adolph, who also became a distinguished biologist, Murie paddled their homemade canoe up and down the Red River near his home in Moorhead, Minnesota, looking for bird nests while keeping an eye out for imaginary Indians — good training, it would turn out, for his future work.

After high school, he enrolled in Fargo College, across the river in North Dakota. Money was short, graduation uncertain. But when his biology professor, Dr. A. M. Bean, took a new teaching position in Oregon, he wrangled an assistantship for his most ambitious student. In 1912, at the age of twenty-three, Murie graduated from Pacific University. During World War I, he would have his nerves tested in the Army balloon service, whose observers, suspended from large and bulbous targets, studied enemy lines. Ten years later, he would earn a Master of Science degree from the University of Michigan, and he eventually received an honorary doctorate from his alma mater of undergraduate years. For the time being, however, he began his thirty-year profession as a field biologist by collecting specimens and taking wildlife photographs for the Oregon State Game Warden. It was not a prestigious job, but it was a job, the first in his chosen field, and he was learning the skills that would make a distinguished career possible. When a break came two years later, he was still young, relatively inexperienced but eager, and there were no entanglements to hold him back. The Carnegie Museum in Pittsburgh had hired a collector to accompany explorations in subarctic Canada, but the man weighed the dangers against family responsibilities and backed out. Would Murie like to go in his place? Of course he would.

The expedition, consisting of an ornithologist leader and Murie as assistant, stepped off the train near the southern end of Hudson Bay, where they met their two Ojibway guides. "I looked around," the young biologist remembers. "We were on the bank of a river thickly flanked by spruce forest as far as one could see. . . . Before us, stretching far into the north, lay the unknown."

Then they got into their canoe to spend the summer paddling north through the blank spaces on their map.

At one point they beached on a barren island in Hudson Bay to prepare bird specimens and rest from hours of fighting a head wind. Far from routes traveled by Indians, in this brief respite the tiny expedition nearly met its end. After the four had stretched their legs a bit, they looked up to see the canoe gliding away high in the water. Impulsively, Murie plunged in, only to feel that "a deadly chill was creeping over me as I floundered in the icy water" of the subarctic sea. A cramp gripped a leg as the canoe skimmed blithely off before the wind. He barely made it back. Meanwhile, the two Indians were busy lashing together drift logs with a bit of wire that happened to be in the skinning outfit. They managed to retrieve their primary means of survival, which had blown against another island.

For all the dangers, he revelled in the experience. In the fall the expedition officially ended, but he stayed on in the north, traveling with Eskimos and Cree Indians on their winter hunts over the snowbound muskeg. Temperatures of forty degrees below zero brought out both his endurance and sensitivity. "There was a feeling of purity about the whole thing," he says wandering about in a frigid night, "as if I were in a holy place...." Echoing Enos Mills, he called what others looked on as harsh and uncivilized a "wonderland."

Two years later, in the spring of 1917, Olaus Murie again struck out by canoe for the Carnegie Museum, this time up the Ste. Marguerite River. The goal of the little band was to become the first scientific expedition to cross Labrador from the St. Lawrence River north to Ft. Chimo, a trading post near the Arctic Circle. From the end of May through the middle of August the group met three people, an Indian carrying a canoe, followed by his wife with their baby in her pack. Again, maps were inaccurate or nonex-

Olaus Murie and a favorite sled dog, Jack, in 1922. Margaret Murie.

istent. For seven hundred and fifty miles they paddled and portaged, losing their way in Labrador's labyrinth of river systems. At one point the Indian guides threatened mutiny. But to Murie wildlife was the main excitement: "All at once I found the place alive with birds. A ruby-crowned kinglet appeared.... He came up close, showing his ruby crown and his bright white-ringed eye. At intervals he sang and I could see his throat vibrate...," he records in his diary as a highlight of the trip.

Though he might not have been consciously aware of the fact, by the time he was thirty Murie had added impressive skills to his college training. He was adept at collecting, he could speak Eskimo, and most importantly he had proved that he could do scientific work in the inhospitable northland. The U.S. Biological Survey, since renamed the Fish and Wildlife Service, sent him to Alaska in 1920. Despite frantic gold rushes, fishing and lumber industries, there were great gaps in solid information about the territory, in the nation's possession for less than sixty years. Areas as large as some states in the lower forty-eight were practically unknown.

Geography at least stays put. Less was known about Alaska's wildlife. In a country hard on most barnyard species, natives as well as white men depended on the wandering caribou for much of their food supply. Declining herds meant hardship, if not starvation, in the north. For six years — by dogteam, on snowshoes, by river steamer — Murie crisscrossed Alaska, serving as a fur warden, studying the brown bear, banding waterfowl. The duties were incidental to his main assignment: probing the dynamics of Alaska's caribou. The result, *Alaska-Yukon Caribou* (1935), remains a standard text for mammalogists.

Romance is difficult in Alaska, at least it was in the days when hunter or biologist might be gone in the wilderness for months at a time. But at 2:30 on a summer

morning in the little log church of Anvik, Margaret
Thomas, carrying a bouquet of arctic poppies, married
Olaus Murie.

As field biologists will testify, the choice of a wife is
particularly crucial. Some friends of the couple considered
Murie's work and doubted that the marriage would last.
They didn't count on the spunk of Mrs. Murie, the first
woman graduate of the University of Alaska. Nor did they
count on her own joy in wilderness, or her love for her
husband. The first day of their marriage, "we suddenly
looked at each other with laughing eyes, knowing that we
were together and ready for anything." Hundreds of miles
from the nearest pediatrician or marriage counselor, they
worked as a team. When a baby came, they took it along on
trips, feeding it powdered milk mixed with water from the
Yukon River. In 1962 Margaret Murie captured the ruggedness and charm of their experiences with *Two in the
Far North,* a book illustrated by her husband.

Pleased with his work on Alaska's caribou, in 1927 the
Biological Survey sent him to Jackson Hole, Wyoming, to
investigate the famous but dwindling elk herd that
ranged near the Tetons. As with the caribou, the elk were
suffering from the pressures of modern civilization. The
present herd owes its health to Murie's meticulous study
and recommendations. In 1945 he retired. He had com-
pleted significant work on mammals during government
service, but his career as a federal employee is unique
beyond that.

Unlike Aldo Leopold, who quit the Forest Service when
bureaucratic frustration threatened to overwhelm his talents, Murie stayed on, attempting to sway official policies.
During his twenty-five years of service, the drive to man-
ipulate nature reached the proportions of a frenetic religious belief. Apparently the government's goal was to turn
the nation's remaining wild areas into an "open-air zoo,"
in the words of one historian, with all the deer hunters

wanted, but no wolves to trouble them, with hydroelectric plants churning out electricity, and neat rows of Douglas firs marching into infinity, ripening for the axe. At a new height of government persecution of the wolf, grizzly bear, and coyote, of damming, clearcutting, and fire suppression, Murie understood, as his supervisors did not, that their Faustian plans would lead to ultimate collapse of ecosystems, that the best way to deal with nature was to leave it alone. During Murie's career, government trappers outnumbered field scientists by a ratio of more than ten to one, and few professional biologists saw the long-term mistakes, or, if they did, were willing to risk their superiors' frowns. There was a bureaucratic, if perverse, wisdom in pulling nature's strings. Manipulation creates jobs, complex programs, the ever larger and more impressive budgets that seem to signal an agency's success, while leaving nature alone asks an unglamorous, if sensitive, patience.

Obviously talented, respected for his thoroughness, and personally likable, nevertheless Olaus Murie had often found himself in the uneasy position of the bureaucratic nonconformist. Donald Worster comments on his career: "...he somehow managed to stand free of the official game-production philosophy, playing the role of a tolerated but unheeded maverick. It could not have been easy for such a peaceable man to be on the outs with so many of his colleagues for so long. He was fierce enough, however, to persist over those two decades in his efforts to convert the Bureau from an anti-predator prejudice to 'the ecological view.' " Though a gentle man, his beliefs marked him a heretic, an iconoclast of official images when he observed that normally mice, not mutton, make up a coyote's diet, or when he urged his chief that "sympathy should be felt for wildlife in general and that we should make greater effort to find what *good* there might be in some species which have ill repute." To the Bureau, however, good

Olaus Murie, about 1950. Margaret Murie.

predators remained dead predators. The agency carefully misplaced his letters, memoranda, and scientific papers, while it devoted ever larger sums of taxpayer dollars to poisoning the land and sending Piper Cubs armed with sharpshooters into the skies over the public's domain.

Yet it does not seem to be entirely true, as Worster maintains, that "his two decades of protest had not had much real effect." For one thing, the agency's fear of Murie grew with his expanding reputation among wildlife specialists. In one case at least, it forbade him from speaking at a wildlife conference — a sign that the Bureau was going on the defensive. Murie's persistent chipping away at official policy not only encouraged dissent on the part of other bureaucrats, it also provided ammunition for such professional groups as the Society of Mammalogists in their struggle for more enlightened government policies toward wildlife. During these stormy years Murie also helped to convert his friend Aldo Leopold from a utilitarian to a holistic approach to nature — a shift with immeasurable benefits to conservation.

Others — Stephen Mather as first head of the National Park Service or Edward Abbey as vituperative novelist — will be honored for contributions in specific areas. But as explorer, government biologist, artist, writer, and leader of one of the country's most aggressive environmental groups, Murie's influence is not easily tallied. In retirement began the fulfillment of his talents and potential leadership. He had the time to follow interests — writing, leading, lecturing, sketching — once held in check by long days and nights in the field. For the next twenty years the Muries' log cabin on the banks of the Snake River was a focus, something of a Mecca, of American conservation. Though at home alone in the wilderness, Murie also thrived in an atmosphere of people involved in a common cause. His guest cabins harbored environmentalists on pilgrimage to Moose, Wyoming, for consultation and relaxation. "We love people," said his wife. "In summer they come from all parts of the world to see us. And the young ones! We're so grateful to have them." A founder of the Wilderness Society ten years earlier, he now served it as director and president. An international authority on wildlife, he traveled to Norway, British Columbia, New Zealand, and South America, advising governments on habitat preservation and the restoration of threatened species. *The Elk of North America* (1951) joined his earlier writings as a necessary text and won the Wildlife Society Award. His *Field Guide to Animal Tracks* (1954) became a unique aid for amateurs and professionals alike in identifying wildlife. Scores of Murie articles, often accompanied by his drawings, appeared in *Audubon, The Living Wilderness,* and *American Forests,* calling attention to threatened wilderness remnants, warning that the grizzly bear, mountain lion, and golden eagle were on their way to extinction unless the public roused itself to insist that the government change its policies of extermination and of habitat destruction. All the while he constantly illustrated books, his own and his wife's, his brother Adolph Murie's classic *The Wolves of Mount McKinley,* and J. Frank Dobie's *The Voice of the Coyote,* an authoritative compilation of coyote lore by one of the West's most popular writers. Catching wind of Murie's growing public stature, *Life* featured the aging champion of preservation in several pages of wilderness photographs. Somewhat inaccurately, if not bombastically, the magazine proclaimed him "a 20th Century Thoreau" and placed him in the tradition of "ancient holy men" seeking peace and "answers to life's mysteries" through nature.

His greatest contribution is the direction he gave to the conservation movement during a critical period. After World War II, the country revelled in the abundance and ease promised by technology and economic expansion. Seemingly, the nation could turn the earth's resources to any ends it desired. From the perspective of thirty-five years it is easier to see the darker side of the promise, the deception involved in the optimism of the time. Along with Robert Marshall, Howard Zahniser, Aldo Leopold, and a handful of other visionaries, Murie recognized that the world was rushing into change faster than it could understand the long-term consequences: "Our country, as we have known it, is in danger. Our free running streams, one after another, are to be submerged. Rich bottomlands are to be put under water. Roads and engineering structures are to penetrate our recreation areas. . . . Neither national parks nor national forests are held sacred. In

short, our human environment is to be drastically altered,
on a huge scale; the pattern of our culture is to be seriously
affected." To Murie the earth was a living organism, not
an intricate machine to be manipulated arbitrarily for
man's pleasures. He distrusted the technological boosterism, the coming age of the computer with its blind faith
that truth could be defined by an endless production of
statistics.

The mechanistic attitude was an acceleration of the
spirit he had seen at work during his government days
with the Biological Survey. Where others saw happiness
based on affluence, he saw problems. In 1949 he warned:
"Up to now we have had a vast unoccupied country. There
has been plenty of room. We have not heard much about
primitive areas, or wilderness. Until recently we have not
had to be much concerned about such matters.... [Now] we
are living in a new world. We are harassed by a multipli-
city of new problems. The world is becoming crowded. We
hear the rumblings of the world population pressure —
the need for food production. Much of this concerns material resources — for the mechanics of peaceful living as well
as for waging possible war. Our civilization is confused,
groping." Even then, as government agencies do today,
the Bureau of Reclamation was justifying a series of dams
by comparing projected financial benefits against the dollar values it assigned to trees and animals of the ecosystems to be sacrificed. At a hearing in Sheridan, Wyoming,
he protested a dam which would flood the Cloud Peak
Primitive Area, pointing out the failure in the agency's
logic: "It appears to me that you and your associated
agencies are trying to balance two unlike things, and from
the wrong base datum. Let us take wildlife as an example.
A dollar value is placed on animals of an area.... So an elk,
we will say, is worth so much. To whom? Solely the people
who sell groceries in the area, gas, or what not. . .? The
figures must be purely accidental and incidental."

The former explorer knew that he could not single-handedly turn the country's precipitous rush into development. What he could do was spend his last years inspiring others to save as much as they could of the nation's natural habitat. To him the measure of a civilization's humanity lay not in its profusion of gadgetry but in the generosity, enlightenment, the care for the earth and concern for its own future it showed in preserving, rather than dominating, nature. To this end he bent himself as president and director of the Wilderness Society, bringing to bear his substantial professional reputation. Several decades before, Aldo Leopold had persuaded the Forest Service to set aside part of the Gila National Forest in New Mexico to be left in a pristine condition. Since then it and sister agencies had designated other "primitive" parcels as preserves. Yet they had remained intact at the whims of the agencies concerned. Murie campaigned for passage of the Wilderness Act, which would grant them permanent protection under Congressional mandate. On the other hand, he recognized a more immediate danger. Having fallen under the influence of timber and mining interests, the government was whittling away at the preserves, opening them to exploitation before passage of the act could protect them. Under such pressure, for instance, the Forest Service proposed to lop off one-third of the Gila Primitive Area.

Murie rushed into the breaches opening throughout the West, testifying, lobbying, heightening public awareness of what it was about to lose forever from the natural legacy. As a result, he deserves substantial credit for saving the choice wilderness areas that today form the West's pristine heritage: San Gorgonio (California); Selway-Bitterroot (Idaho and Montana); Three Sisters (Oregon); Cloud Peak (Wyoming); and many others. He fought off incursions by the Army on Olympic National Park and with William O. Douglas promoted preservation in the Cascades. Working through the Wilderness Society, he piqued public awareness to halt the Rampart Dam on Alaska's Yukon River and the Narrows Dam proposed for the mouth of Snake River Canyon. At the age of sixty-seven he led an expedition to the Brooks Range, spurring the Secretary of Interior to set aside the vast Arctic Wildlife Refuge in northeastern Alaska. However, he was unable to enjoy his last success. His wife remembers, "As for the Wilderness Act, that was an eight-year struggle and I don't know how many hearings Olaus attended, how many articles he wrote, how many letters (though during part of this period he was ill and in hospital...). I can't possibly list all the lectures and speeches Olaus made...." One year after his death in 1963 the act making permanent preservation official government policy passed Congress.

When he died, magazines and newspapers from Connecticut to Alaska praised him as "one of the greatest naturalists of this continent" and as "the one person who best personified wilderness in our culture." Yet his influence went far beyond the visible accomplishments. There is a photograph of Murie that tells more about him than a list of his publications or a summary of his awards. The biologist is dancing with a group of Aleuts, arms raised, smiling. The spontaneity comes through the snapshot: this is no civilized white on a condescending lark with the local natives, but a man sharing a central joy. He reflected on his career that "the happiest experience of all [was] getting acquainted with the people." But Murie was no sentimental pushover. Once during their courtship, his future wife snapped at his "everlasting good nature." His response: "Look, if you want a fight, you can have it." Beneath the warmth, she assures, "was steel within," the strength combined with sympathy that made him an effective activist and sparked inspiration in others. Remembering their friendship, one man rendered the ultimate praise, "It made me a better man."

Olaus Murie's life began before the invention of the automobile and ended after Hiroshima. He recognized the deception of an age that offered a lavish degree of physical comfort in some areas but at the price of overcrowding, pollution, and constant spiritual frustration. His view of society is best summed up in a comment he made on Eskimo friends, who each winter faced the possibility of starvation: "As I think of my sojourn among the Eskimos of Hudson Bay, I realize that there was no law there — no officers in uniform. People reacted to each other in a natural way. We, as humans, have certainly not reached our human goal; we are only on the way. I am convinced that in the evolution of the human spirit something much worse than hunger can happen to a people."

Joseph Wood Krutch with owl. Arizona Historical Society.

Chapter 11

Joseph Wood Krutch:
Quiet Voice For
"The Devil's Domain"

I stood in the glare of the warm exhaust turning red;
around our group I could hear the wilderness listen.

I thought hard for us all. . . .
— William Stafford

At the corner of Grant and Swan, customers in Dunkin' Donuts tend to their coffee and stare dully out at the pine-topped Santa Catalina Mountains. Each year the peaks recede farther into the aerial scum produced by the Southwest's fastest growing city. Across the street is an anomaly, several acres of creosote bush and cactus hemmed in by a shopping center, a trailer court, and subdivisions. A realtor's prize, some may think; the plot was the home of America's most eloquent speaker for desert preservation. Twenty years ago he wandered here when the city was miles away, watching the migrations of the pileated warbler, marveling at Scorpio, known as the Hand of God to the local Papago Indians, "straggling downward in the southern sky." Year after year Tucson

131

grew toward him, and "he was heartbroken to see it," says his widow, who still lives on the little patch of desert in the middle of urban sprawl. Individually, many Americans have felt heartbreak at the loss of familiar surroundings, yet the public attitudes that fuel modern expansion go back to the nation's origins.

Early settlers battling to stay alive in the gloomy forests along the Atlantic seaboard compared their plight to that of Israelites wandering in the "howling wilderness" of the Bible. To them, according to Paul Brooks, the woods inhabited by wild beasts and marauding Indians "was a place of temptation, the Devil's domain. To subdue it was not only a practical necessity, it was holy work." Their struggle to hack permanent communities out of vegetative chaos was harsh enough, yet little did settlers anticipate what lay ahead on the other side of the waste of trees. When over two centuries later they reached the arid regions beyond the Mississippi — where a man had to "dig for wood and climb for water," where "everything has either horns or thorns," as the popular sayings go — they must have felt that they had passed through the very gates of hell. Cattle died of thirst, crops turned to dust; the sun went over day after rainless day with maddening regularity. Unable to adjust to the new circumstances, some pioneers simply went out of their minds.

Today conservationists are fighting to preserve the remnants of America's forest and desert wilderness. However, given the backbreaking economic realities and a pattern of settlement that cast each man out on his own resources, it's no wonder that early pioneers showed little sensitivity toward untamed nature and passed their attitudes along to more prosperous generations. In the nineteenth century, a few writers such as Thoreau caught the literary public's fancy with their celebrations of wild nature, but readers gave lip service to their views more as pleasant escapism than as workable approaches to the environment. Not until the turn of the century, when the wilderness was all but gone, did a relatively secure and comfortable life permit serious reevaluation of attitudes toward the natural heritage. Less fearful of raving lions and rampaging Indians, some sons and daughters of the frontiersmen looked about them, took a deep breath, and saw the folklore, the history, the plants and animals that their parents had missed in their frenetic efforts to stay alive. Such novelists as Mary Hunter Austin, Willa Cather, and Zane Grey considered pristine mountains and plains as essential to what they viewed as a unique and profound Western experience. If many early novels about the West tend to have improbably romantic plots, they come closer to social realities by emphasizing nature as a healing balm for recently overcivilized man. From that position it was only one step for more recent authors to raise their readers' sensitivity. Aldo Leopold and Joseph Wood Krutch helped the public to see wilderness as having value, not only economically and aesthetically, but also — in the current terminology — for itself. And from there it was just one further though belated step to demands for preservation of a precious and fading legacy.

Deserts stretch around the Rocky Mountains from the Mexican border to the state of Washington. To put it statistically, about 75% of the land west of the Mississippi receives less than twenty inches of precipitation a year, a fact that John Wesley Powell pointed out to a stunned Congress in 1878. In recent years, Joseph Wood Krutch probably did more than any other writer to change society's view of what it had long looked on as undifferentiated wasteland. But he came to his own appreciation of the arid region late in life and, like many conservationists, by an improbable route. When he finally did come to an understanding of desert areas, he brought with him a perception of America that had been maturing for fifty years.

Born in 1893 in Knoxville, Tennessee, he majored in mathematics at the local state university. However, the son of a merchant soon had enough of farmers snoring in their wagons around the public square the night before market day. After graduation he fled to what he took to be the dazzling Babylon of New York. Krutch might have been Knoxville's maverick, reflecting a strain of nonconformity traceable to a line of German nobles, but in New York he was no profligate son. Abandoning mathematics, he earned his M.A. degree in the humanities from Columbia University. In 1924 he received his Ph.D. in literature and married a French Basque nurse visiting relatives in the United States.

Over the next twenty-five years, Krutch's career reflects the successful urbanity of the Knoxville boy. He taught English and journalism at prestigious Columbia, where he established lifelong friendships with such academic lights as Mark Van Doren. In the city that considers itself the very center of the nation's culture, he became a luminary in his own right, serving as drama critic of *The Nation* in the liberal magazine's heyday.

Publishers brought out his scholarly works on an impressive variety of subjects: Boccaccio, Cervantes, Samuel Johnson, Poe, Proust, Stendhal. One volume foreshadows his later concern for conservation. On the very eve of the Great Depression, he published his most controversial book, *The Modern Temper* (1929). This series of essays rejected the wild optimism based on blind faith in science fashionable in the Twenties. Except for this book, and a sensitive study of Thoreau in 1948, there was hardly a hint of the future environmentalist in Krutch; he was the brilliant country boy successful in a sophisticated literary world.

With middle age came an epiphany. More to indulge his wife than to please himself, for years Krutch had divided his time between the city and a country home in Redding,

Sonoran Desert. To the shock of sophisticated city friends, Krutch suddenly left New York, "to get away from the crowds, to get air I could breathe and for the natural beauty of the desert."
Ann and Myron Sutton.

Connecticut. One winter night after completing the Thoreau book, he sat reading a nature essay, "...and it suddenly occurred to me for the first time to wonder if I could do something of the sort." In his imagination he heard New England's traditional announcement of warm weather, the chirpings of a little frog known as the spring peeper. He wrote:

> Surely one day a year might be set aside on which to celebrate our ancient loyalties and to remember our ancient origins. And I know of none more suitable for that purpose than the Day of the Peepers. "Spring is come!", I say when I hear them, and: "The most ancient of Christs has risen!" But I also add something which, for me at least, is more important. "Don't forget," I whisper to the peepers: "we are all in this together."

The words delighted him with their contrast to the "serious and rather solemn" prose of his scholarly books. He went on to complete *The Twelve Seasons,* a series of whimsical essays, one for each month.

But for three factors Joseph Wood Krutch might have spent the rest of his life penning gentle nature pieces about New England, but even rural Connecticut is not as rural as a nature writer with developing sensibilities might wish. To the shock of sophisticated city friends, in 1950 he retired from teaching, packed, and moved to Tucson, Arizona. His explanation was blunt: "I came for three reasons: to get away from New York and the crowds, to get air I could breathe and for the natural beauty of the desert and its wildlife." He settled on the outskirts of Tucson, then a small, quiet city, and published one book — sometimes two — a year on the arid heritage he was exploring in Arizona and surrounding states. While his popularity as a nature essayist grew, so did abuse of the deserts he loved. The activism of Defenders of Wildlife and the Sierra

Club won his support, and local scientists persuaded Krutch to become a trustee of the newly founded Arizona-Sonora Desert Museum, an office he held for twenty years. In the Sixties, NBC recognized the growing public concern for the environment by broadcasting three television specials featuring Joseph Wood Krutch on tour of the Grand Canyon and the Sonoran and Baja deserts.

Yet, unlike his stormy contemporary, Bernard DeVoto, for the most part Joseph Wood Krutch was a shy, introverted man, not fond of meetings and not the type to mount the barricades for the threatened land. Instead, he preferred to write about his personal fascination with nature. His relationships with desert life were private and essentially religious — if that word is applied to what inspires wonder, that gives shape and definition to a person's life. The beauty of his later writings lies in insights that re-create the freshness and clarity of the author's original experiences. Krutch was teaching his readers to see with new eyes.

His first book on the Southwest, *The Desert Year* (1952), described the delicate but powerful drama of the approaching monsoon season. Krutch marveled at the complicated chemistry that triggers cactus seeds precisely when temperature and moisture conditions are most favorable. Armed with a flashlight, he strolled through the washes and mesquite, telling in almost mystical terms in *The Voice of the Desert* (1954) about the strange nocturnal flutterings of the Pronuba moth around the yucca plant.

In the revelations about desert life that he shared with a nationwide audience he saw a lesson. On deserts, "life is everywhere precarious, man everywhere small." Yet technological civilization is a blind alley; especially in the fragile arid regions, man is destroying the very land that sustains him in order to surround himself with abundance. "Abundance of what?" Krutch asked. Do more freeways, more highrises, more television sets make people happier?

A travel book on Baja, *The Forgotten Peninsula* (1961), concretized his position. In Lower California he saw virtue in an economy of scarcity, where people carefully used and reused resources. He had said earlier, "I am no ascetic and, so at least I believe, no fanatic of any other sort. I am not praising want and I have no romantic notion that distresses should not be relieved." To Krutch, poverty that robbed people of their dignity was not picturesque. However, in rural Baja the scattered population lived in a healthy balance with the environment. The writer pointed out that the worst social problems occurred in the northern part of the Mexican state, where masses of Anglo tourists crowded the spreading network of paved roads. Along with the influx came not only a disrupted life for the local people but permanent destruction of their heritage: "One after another the most accessible mountains and beaches are turning into Coney Islands of horror...." In Mexico, as well as in the rest of the world, man had laid a trap for himself — and he was falling into it. In its drive for progress, Western civilization had abandoned primitivism and saw uncontrolled technological development as its only goal. Krutch knew that technology could serve society, but he felt that man lacked the wisdom to keep it from becoming a mindless tyrant.

Some years before he died in 1970, the former Columbia professor of English chuckled about his amateur status as a scientist: "I probably know more about plants than any other drama critic and more about the theater than any botanist." However, some scientists are quick to fault his books, particularly for their anthropomorphism. While he lived, other critics claimed that the state of human affairs did not justify Krutch's doubts about modern civilization. In the final analysis, Krutch's finely drawn musings are more reflective than objectively scientific, full of wonder at nature and questionings of man's overconfident but tenuous position in it. Whatever its real or imagined faults, there is a good deal of truth in his approach. In less than a decade since his death, fears have grown over the future of the Southwest. As its sprawling cities come to resemble Los Angeles, as agriculture despairs over failing wells, as its once celebrated air becomes more clogged each year with industrial litter, the general public is becoming alarmed that the arid region may not be able to sustain an economy traditionally based on waste and unlimited growth, thus giving credence to the warnings of the shy and concerned desert lover.

William O. Douglas. Library of Congress, William O. Douglas.

Chapter 12

Should Trees have Rights?: William O. Douglas Expands the Law

Still
The world out-Herods Herod....

Robert Lowell

When the distinguished American official came trudging in from the desert, Iranians eyed him with suspicion. What had he been up to prowling around in their stony wilderness? Out conferring with the famous General Lincoln, who happened to be leading U.S. troops through their territory, was the deadpan reply. Soon cables were flying between Teheran and Washington. Grim CIA agents swooped in to join the Iranian Army in hunting down the renegade Lincoln.

The spoof was part of his humor. A nonconformist during one of America's most rigid periods of conformity, he knew that a person couldn't take life too seriously if he were to keep his ideals and still survive. He had spent a good part of his youth riding the rails. He knew the icy

141

feeling of being shot at by police. He had arrived at Columbia Law School with six cents in his pocket. Three times in later years opponents roiled the political waters in movements to impeach him. As a result of his background, William O. Douglas spoke for the underdog. To him America's trees, rivers, and mountains belonged in that category because they had few supporters willing to stand up in their defense. For them he articulated one of the most progressive environmental concepts of recent times: that the natural world should have legal rights. The idea is a capstone in the development of conservation thinking. While environmentalists applauded, exploiters and mossbacks howled with derision.

During his boyhood, doctors were helpless in the face of polio. The disease often killed or left its victims crippled for life. In 1901, at the age of three, Douglas felt his legs go numb until "they seemed almost detached, the property of someone else." The country doctor could do little. He recommended massages with salt water. Day after day the boy's mother kneaded the shrunken muscles.

As it turned out, he was among the fortunate. Months later the boy learned to walk again on his spindly legs. But the disease left scars. When Douglas reached his teens, he couldn't bear the snickering of schoolmates at the pipestems that the traditional knee breeches of the day made a constant subject for ridicule. Added to this, his father, an itinerant Presbyterian minister, died before the boy was six. The proud family was forced to live on the wrong side of Yakima's tracks. Without a successful day of scavenging in alleys and garbage cans for a few penniesworth of junk, the two brothers and a sister might go without food.

The boy became a loner. After a day of excelling at school, he'd cross the Northern Pacific's bridge, pass through the camps of the hoboes and Wobblies, and disappear into the foothills north of Yakima. On excursions over Mount Adams and Mount Rainier, he didn't walk —

he ran — sometimes vomiting after the strain, but the muscles stretched and grew firm. Years later his speed, whether over the Himalayas or in the woods around Washington, D.C., was a steady five miles an hour, a match for his intellectual pace. Few could keep up in either category.

There is something Whitmanesque, something typically American, in the roughness and vision of his early years. Looking down on the lights of Yakima, feeling the warm chinook wind on his cheek, he sensed the "kindliness of the universe to man," the "health and strength and courage" of the earth. In contrast, he saw the ugliness of life in town. A lawyer had squandered his father's life-insurance money, leaving the Douglas family destitute. When he was a naive teen-ager, a self-righteous reformer hired him to spy along the brothels of Front Street. He saw his own poverty reflected in the people he met. As much as the family needed the income, he quit in shame: "In time I came to feel a warmth for all these miserable people, something I never felt for the high churchman who hired me. What orphanages had turned them out? Which of them had turned to prostitution and bootlegging as a result of grinding poverty?" The words became a theme for his career. The future Supreme Court justice knew from hard experience that "he who has a long purse will always have a lawyer, while the indigent will be without one." The heroes of his youth were the progressive leaders of the day: Hiram Johnson, reform governor of California; William Borah, senator from Idaho; and Gifford Pinchot of the Forest Service — those who formed a counter tradition of responsibility both toward nature and their fellowmen.

Whitman College offered a tuition scholarship, and September, 1916, found the high school valedictorian pumping his bicycle the 165 miles to Walla Walla. Four years later the new baccalaureate was teaching English, Latin, and public speaking, and leading Boy Scouts on forays from his home town. His mother, feeling a modicum of financial comfort for the first time in years, wanted him to secure the family's future by becoming a high school principal, but the young teacher was restless. He spent off hours in Yakima's federal courtroom. Watching the local lawyers perform, he decided he could "be a match for any of them."

In 1922 Columbia Law School sent the Westerner a letter of acceptance. It was long before the days of the massive work-study programs and government loans that now help students. Columbia would admit him, but he'd have to make it on his own, far from his home. Furthermore, he'd first have to cross the continent without digging too deeply into the seventy-five dollars he'd saved. Luck was with him. A Yakima firm wanted someone to escort two thousand sheep to market. He hopped a freight to Wenatchee, Washington, rendezvoused with the milling creatures, and "rode in style in the caboose," all the way to Chicago. Like Bernard DeVoto leaving Ogden, Utah, at about the same time for Northwestern University, Douglas had dreams but not much else. As the sun set, he climbed to the top of the car and felt the tug of the orchards and sagebrush country flying past. He also knew the exhilaration of escape from "a dull and listless life," a sense of "going into battle in a strange and faraway place."

With his bleating charges safely delivered in Chicago, Douglas hitched a ride on a boxcar to the East, arriving in New York "hungry, dead-tired, homesick, broke, and bruised." Three years later, armed with his law degree, he was working for a Wall Street firm. Then Yale asked him to join its faculty. In a few years Douglas had made a name for himself in the specialties of corporate finance and bankruptcy — the latter a booming field after the Crash of 1929. Private institutions and government agencies hired him to study the economic paralysis of the world's richest nation.

In 1936 President Roosevelt appointed him to the Securities and Exchange Commission. Two years later he was its chairman, responsible in part for bringing order to the nation's chaotic financial sustem. From Washington, D.C., he saw on a larger scale the same corruption and exploitation that had disgusted him in Yakima. To put a stop to the scandals that had preceded the Depression, he reorganized the New York Stock Exchange. His new SEC regulations offered protection to the country's small investors — who reminded Douglas of the Cascades' golden-mantled ground squirrel: numerous and easily preyed upon.

It was a rough, exposed job, but he showed financiers that he had instituted a new order. At a large dinner in New York, the SEC chairman bluntly told the "masters of Wall Street" that they were "still fighting for opportunities to exploit the unsuspecting public," and assured them that his job was "to make sure they did not succeed." Honesty made enemies, but Douglas pressed the work, proud of the example that his staff was setting for the country's businessmen. As a matter of policy, his eighteen hundred men and women politely turned down all industry invitations for free lunches and weekends on yachts. His straightforward style caught the eye of Franklin Delano Roosevelt, who was holding the shaking system together with his New Deal. One spring Sunday in 1939 a caddie with a message from the President came puffing up to a foursome at the Manoe Country Club. As usual Douglas was busy scheming to win his weekly fifty cents; he always managed to talk partners into a few handicap strokes. But this game would have to wait. Justice Brandeis had retired, and Roosevelt wanted a Westerner to give geographical balance to the Supreme Court. Dumbfounded, the man who not many years earlier had chaperoned a trainload of sheep on his way to school began a service of thirty-six years on the bench, the longest, and certainly one of the most controversial, terms in the Court's history.

His success throughout his active, stormy life was due perhaps as much to the good fortune that came his way as to his brilliance and drive. The early bout with polio left him scarred but determined. Once, because he couldn't pay the dollar bribe to stay aboard, a conductor forced him to jump into the darkness from a speeding freight. The iron arm of a switch nearly impaled him. Luck was with him again in 1949. A horse pitched the fifty-year-old Justice off a trail in the Cascades, then came rolling down over him. The accident broke all his ribs except one, but Douglas recovered. In 1970 Gerald Ford, Spiro Agnew, and Richard Nixon fueled the last effort to impeach him. As evidence of his improprieties, they offered a belligerent but not very good Douglas book, *Points of Rebellion* (1970), whose sales were lagging. After a Ford ally stormed at the work from the floor of the House of Representatives, its sales shot up tenfold. In retrospect, at least, it seems that Douglas is one of those periodically brought to the brink, only to be plucked back chuckling and strengthened, if not richer.

All his life the Justice couldn't exist without wilderness; "a driving force" compelled him into America's mountains. Yet with other hikers, especially after World War II, he saw clear cuts, dams, highways — the blind destruction of what he had loved from boyhood. "Man took the wealth and left only the ashes of the wondrous earth for those who followed," he observed. His high position in Washington gave him a unique opportunity to see the process at work and to do something about it. Just as in his SEC days, when he accused the political and economic system that tended to benefit influential insiders, he saw that "the public domain was up for grabs and its riches were being dispersed by the federal bureaucracy to a favored few." To him a stand for conservation grew naturally from his broad commitment to civil rights applied equally to all. And that meant not universal exploitation, but preservation; future generations had their rights too.

Many of his more than twenty-five books, for example *A Wilderness Bill of Rights* (1965) and *Farewell to Texas: A Vanishing Wilderness* (1967), deal with the country's natural heritage and the national shame of its loss. But he went beyond writing. Though opponents criticized him for his liberal interpretations of the Bill of Rights — and for a succession of four attractive and youthful wives — Douglas enjoyed his role as maverick among Washington's conformists. In all likelihood to his own delight, they added to their list of "improprieties" his activism for the environment. Often in scuffed boots and a battered Western hat, he marched with other conservationists. He spoke in favor of salmon and Canada geese and against dams on the Columbia River; in favor of protecting the Wind River Mountains from poisoning by the Fish and Wildlife Service; in favor of natural forests and against Park Service designs to build cities in Yellowstone. Waving to TV cameras, he joined Olaus Murie on a 180-mile protest hike down the right-of-way of the old C & O canal outside Washington, D.C., and saved the green strip from freeway builders. Perhaps not since Gifford Pinchot had a high government official dared to take such exposed positions for the environment. In 1910 President Taft had fired Pinchot for the risk. Impeachment, however, is needed to remove a Court Justice — a tactic that the opposition never was able to bring off.

Despite effective activism, Douglas' most original and enduring contribution to conservation is in jurisprudence: the assertion that natural objects should have legal rights. His dissent in *Sierra Club* v. *Morton* embedded in the legal tradition an attitude going back at least to Thoreau and Muir in the last century and set forth by Aldo Leopold's "Land Ethic" in this one. It is a culmination in environmental thinking, a shift from Pinchot's early utilitarianism to the expanded view that man should live in harmony with nature rather than devote his energies to exploiting it. Furthermore, as is of utmost importance in the courtroom, the concept is based on a long and solid line of precedents, many of them taken for granted in business affairs. In strictly legal terms, Justice Douglas saw this legal concept as a tool of environmentalists, so often losing to monied interests, to increase their leverage in defense of the earth.

Gradually over the centuries, civilization has extended rights to the rightless — to women, children, slaves. For the most part, however, a person may do as he wishes with his land. A company may level an entire forest, regardless of consequences to future generations. Yet due to abuse of the earth, civilization now faces the very issue of survival. The solution lies in extending the social conscience from humans to the planet which supports them. Leopold sums up the concept: "The extension of ethics to this... human environment is... an evolutionary possibility and an ecological necessity.... Individual thinkers since the days of Ezekiel and Isaiah have asserted that the despoliation of land is not only inexpedient but wrong. Society, however, has not yet affirmed their belief. I regard the present conservation movement as the embryo of such an affirmation."

The specific legal issue involved "standing" — the right to sue. The Sierra Club went to court to preserve Mineral King Valley, part of Sequoia National Forest, from the twenty ski lifts, ten restaurants, and parking lots proposed by Walt Disney Productions. In 1972 the Supreme Court handed down a four to three decision, ruling that the Club had no legal right to come to the defense of Mineral King. In dissent Douglas pointed out that the issue was not the rights of the Sierra Club, Walt Disney, or the government. The crux of the matter was the right of the valley to exist. The suit should not be called *Sierra Club* v. *Morton* but *Mineral King* v. *Morton* — a shift of perspective that would change the entire complexion of the case.

For purposes of the law, he continued, the courts regularly treat ships and corporations and other inanimate objects as personalities, granting them standing and other rights. Yet ships and corporations are expendable. Why not also extend the rights to the nature on which the country depends for its very existence? "So it would be as respects valleys, alpine meadows, rivers, lakes, estuaries, beaches, ridges, groves of trees, swampland, or even air that feels the destructive pressures of modern technology.... Those people who have a meaningful relation to that body of water — whether it be a fisherman, a canoeist, a zoologist, or a logger — must be able to speak for the values which the river represents and which are threatened with destruction." This thinking has a special beauty in the eyes of environmentalists. If generally accepted by the courts — as seems to be the trend — it would strengthen their legal position as advocates for the earth. Until his retirement in 1975 at the age of seventy-seven, Justice Douglas interpreted the law not as a rigid abstraction but as a reflection of a society's progress.

David Brower. Friends of the Earth.

Chapter 13

David Brower and Charisma:
The Rebirth of the
Conservation Movement

> *...night air still and the rocks*
> *Warm. Sky over endless mountains.*
> *All the junk that goes with being human*
> *Drops away....*
> — Gary Snyder

Part of the general tumult of the 1960's and 1970's was the second growth of conservation into a movement at least as heady as its first surge at the turn of the century. At its center was the Sierra Club, expanding so fast it could hardly keep track of new members. At the center of the Club was a visionary dropout, the quizzical David Brower. Brower, while denouncing the profligate culture, could also hold forth on the esthetic simplicity of a beer can. In 1969, goaded by the famous nature photographer Ansel Adams, the Club's old guard readied itself to fire the executive director for his wayward attempts at greening the nation's oldest environmental group.

His childhood was a mixture of misery and escape. A fall from a baby carriage when he was a year old knocked out his front teeth and damaged his gums. Schoolmates jeered him as "The Toothless Boob." In 1920, when David was eight, his mother went blind. To compound the problems, his father lost his position as an instructor of mechanical drawing at the Berkeley campus of the University of California. The boy peddled papers and helped keep up the family's main source of income, two rundown apartments behind the Brower house. In his freshman year at Berkeley, he hoped to gain a little status and socializing by joining a fraternity. During rush, he saw a membership delegation come up the street, peer at his shabby home, and then pass on.

There were compensations. He wandered the then wild Berkeley Hills gathering rocks for his collections. When he was fifteen, a curious black, white, and green butterfly caught his eye on Grizzly Peak. He had discovered a new species! — a boost for his flagging teen-age ego. Brower still amazes fellow hikers by calling out the names of butterflies swirling ahead over the trail or floating on the thermals along cliffs; he credits his sharp sight to the days when he walked through the Berkeley countryside describing what he saw to his blind mother. Occasionally the family loaded their Maxwell and drove into California's Sierra Nevada. Yet even on vacations, fears dogged him. Perhaps as a result of his scarring childhood fall, the future mountaineer often sat in the car trembling while the others peered over tourist vistas. It took Brower years to settle down. College didn't help the financial and psychological strains. He dropped out as a sophomore to alternate work in a candy factory with trips into the mountains. In 1933 Ansel Adams sponsored his membership in the Sierra Club. Two years later the candy factory fired Brower for his continuing wilderness absences, and he spent the next six years doing office work at Yosemite National Park. There, enthusiasm for the surrounding peaks overcame his fears. By making thirty-three first ascents he earned a reputation as one of the area's most aggressive climbers.

When World War II broke out, he was editing books for the University of California Press. The Army made use of his climbing skills in the Tenth Mountain Division; and in Italy he was awarded the Bronze Star. After the War he went back to editing. Then, in 1952, the Sierra Club chose him as its first full-time executive director, a job that lasted for seventeen years. His career had begun at the age of forty.

To keep its machinery running, the Club had a qualified middle-aged man, who could scale mountains as well as shepherd its occasional publications through the press. Yet Brower had seen change come to the Sierras. He had stood before the Royal Valhalla Motor Lodge, squatted in tinseled glory on a spot near Lake Tahoe where he had camped as a boy. The Club didn't reckon that its board had brought into conjunction a smoldering firebrand and a public again about to seize on conservation with near evangelism.

Under John Muir the Sierra Club had been what he meant it to be — primarily a political lever to preserve the Sierras, secondarily an outing group. However, zeal cooled after the death of its famous founder, and enthusiasm shifted to an elaborate hiking program for the largely well-off, if not wealthy, membership. Doctors, lawyers, and corporation executives — people not usually known for decrying exploitation — served on its board of directors. They led a "posey-picking hiking society," as one thwarted activist called it, "a coterie of gentleman do-gooders," in the words of another. Protests, when made, were feeble and polite, not designed to chafe. In defending the use of Diablo Canyon for a nuclear reactor, Ansel Adams noted: "Diablo, for example, is just another beautiful canyon. There are lots of those." The words of another Club official, a realtor fearful of militancy, summed up the prevailing mood of many conservation organizations of the time: "I believe we can accomplish as much by friendly persuasion. I don't believe in total capitulation of the enemy or pounding your shoe on the table. I don't believe we should be negative. I'm a realtor and I've never sold a house yet by being negative." At the time of the Brower appointment, the Sierra Club had not won a single major environmental battle in the thirty-eight years since Muir's death.

Former Secretary of the Interior Stewart Udall has dubbed David Brower "the most effective single person on the cutting edge of conservation in this country." That probably is the case. But as is true of other effective conservation movers, the new executive director succeeded by taking keen advantage of favorable winds already blowing. After the War, California went through another of its periodic booms, and the restless population drifting West tended to be far more critical and activist than the state's old-timers. Newcomers arrived in search of Eden; instead they found their garden trampled by the new population shift. They wanted to put a stop to this destruction, to make California as idyllic as they had imagined before leaving their homes in the crowded East. Furthermore, the beginning of the nuclear age and such books as Rachel Carson's *Silent Spring* had shocked people across the nation into the awareness that conservation had a direct bearing on their future. The earth was not an infinitely forgiving place. Environmental abuses were bringing down their house around them. Many of them joined the Sierra Club, tame but tinged with a legacy of activism.

As with other movements, frivolous or profound, the environmental trend spread eastward from the West Coast. When Brower took over his new job, the Club had just 7,000 members, most of them in California. When he left in 1969, membership had swollen tenfold to a nationwide total of 70,000, reflecting the general ecological

David Brower playing accordian on the trail. "I have to be an optimist," he says. "Otherwise, I'd open a waffle shop." The Sierra Club.

awakening. Both Brower and the new joiners wanted change. As it happened, he had a rousing issue at hand to unite the clamoring and widespread troops. Government engineers decided to build a dam on the Green River that would back water into Dinosaur National Monument. The scheme sounded ominously like the Hetch Hetchy disaster of forty years earlier, which had violated a National Park by turning one of Yosemite's scenic canyons into a hydroelectric eyesore. Unwittingly the Bureau of Reclamation provided the catalyst that united conservationists across the nation for the first time in decades. Incited by Brower, even the mossbacks stirred themselves for the fight.

Under the clearly righteous banner of Dinosaur, Brower began his innovations. The 1954 book *This Is Dinosaur* was the model for the first of a large format exhibit series that has since opened the public's eyes to its wilderness heritage. The series not only won a name for the Club as a quality publisher but also drew added thousands to its membership. Foremost, though, Brower grasped what gentle nature lovers in the intervening decades since Muir had chosen to ignore: environmental issues are political issues. They are not won by friendly persuasion and pleas to the goodwill of abusers. The new environmentalists stuffed envelopes, wrote their Congressmen, paraded, lobbied, appeared en masse to testify at hearings. The tactics that eventually squelched the dam in Dinosaur showed Brower's followers that only hard-nosed political clout could save the remaining ten percent of the earth not yet eroded, inundated, asphalted, and strip-mined. Redirected by Brower and other leaders, the energy generated by Dinosaur went on to stop dams in the Grand Canyon and create National Parks across the country. In 1964 it gave a final boost to the Wilderness Act. Brower had led the Sierra Club, along with conservation in general, out of the garden club and into the streets and into the halls of Congress.

The phenomenon was not due to well-planned tactics alone. Brower had anticipated the activist mood of the 1960's. Police were clubbing war protestors; the Hare Krishna sang in the streets. The college generation was frothing, blaming those over thirty for the world's sorry state. As he jetted back and forth across the country, his personality — witty, ironic, if not quirky — matched the nation's mood. Brower won a following by what he still calls "The Sermon," leaning "up to the lectern with his feet together and his knees slightly bent, like a skier," as John McPhee describes his performance. Through Brower, audiences saw a vision of coming ecological doom — unless they changed their attitudes toward the earth. According to another Brower observer, Harold Peterson, the "patricianly handsome, disquietingly intense, preternaturally young man of 56 with a magnificent shock of prematurely white hair" not only had faith in the young — the requisite blind faith of leadership — but a bouncy hope for the future. "I *have* to be an optimist," he said. "It keeps me in business. Otherwise, I'd open a waffle shop."

Often he cast his philosophy in witticisms. If not always accurate, they had a racy appeal, and they helped establish a vocabulary of ideas for the new environmentalists:

> Population is pollution spelled inside out.
>
> We don't flood the Sistine Chapel so tourists can get nearer the ceiling.
>
> I am not at all anxious to go back to the Stone Age, but that's where our addiction to growth is sending us.
>
> When rampant growth happens in an individual, we call it cancer.

Brower had taken on the burden of saving the world from itself. To him, hardly anything could be excessive in achieving the goal. Looking around at the Santa Barbara oil spill, at species sliding toward extinction, at the world's dwindling food supply and its burgeoning population, others shared his alarm. As the executive director's zeal approached collision with the staid ruling board, author of *The Population Bomb* Paul Ehrlich warned: "If somebody told me there was a 50-50 chance Brower would destroy the Sierra Club, I'd say go ahead, it's a bargain. The world is going to tumble around its ears if the Sierra Club — or someone — doesn't do a job in the next five years. If the Sierra Club's main worry is the preservation of its own existence, there won't be any environment left for it to exist *in*." Most members shared the outlines of Brower's concerns. One poll indicated that eighty-five percent wanted to move even faster toward his activist goals. Yet fears also grew that Brower's brand of frenetic enthusiasm would wreck the nation's foremost environmental group by rendering it financially insolvent long before it could achieve Brower's ends.

That enthusiasm led him to act without the sanction of the volunteer and slow-moving board. "They want to run this place like a bank," quipped Brower as he shrugged off criticism, then plunged ahead. As popular as the Sierra Club publications were, they lost nearly $300,000. In spite of this, he launched plans not only to add an international series but documentary films, television programs, and advertising campaigns. Providence had always taken care of the Sierra Club; the money would come from somewhere, Brower assured critics.

Tossing salving words over his shoulder, on his own Brower approached large corporations — Xerox and Time-Life — for financing. He wrote checks and signed unauthorized book contracts, one giving him a percentage of the sales. This was not for his own use — while spurring on her husband, Brower's wife continued to live with pans scattered about the house to catch rain dripping through the roof — but to create a discretionary fund beyond the control of the cautious board. Yet his words weren't quieting to those responsible for the everyday solvency of the Club. They recognized Brower's genius for swaying the public, but they also saw a different kind of apocalypse approaching. Commented one appalled official: "There's a recklessness to Dave that's terrifying. It's like driving down a city street with a man who's going 90 miles an hour."

Brower stepped on the gas. He saw the fruits of his activities; people were lying down in the paths of bulldozers, chaining themselves to trees. When issues needed speedy attention, on his own initiative he placed full-page ads in the *New York Times* and the *Washington Post* in the name of the Sierra Club. His blitzkrieg stirred public clamors to save the redwoods from loggers and keep dams out of the Grand Canyon. But the ads cost as much as $20,000 each, and they were blatantly unauthorized by his employers, the Club's board of directors. Furthermore, less than twenty-four hours after the first ad appeared, the Internal Revenue Service announced an investigation

of the Sierra Club. Six months later, because of its activism the Club lost tax-deductible status, a severe financial blow. "Seldom in history," commented the *Nation,*
"has a federal bureaucracy reacted with such cobra-like
speed." To support dams in the Grand Canyon, the Central
Arizona Project Association had spent seven times more
than had Brower — without any stirrings from the government. Clearly the IRS action was a case of selective
enforcement aimed at intimidating those opposing federal
policy.

However, the IRS ploy backfired. A year after its decision, the Sierra Club had gained nearly 10,000 members,
an indication of the public's ecological commitment. Still,
visionary leadership clashed with self-preservation. Ap-
prehensions among Club leaders grew over what the
quixotic Brower might do next. Opponents accused him of
using the same high-handed tactics that he criticized in
the government. A new board of directors elected in the
spring of 1969 forced him to resign, the culmination of a
tense drama watched by the nation's leading newspapers.

The executive director had done what he saw as necessary, but he had moved too fast and too far for an organization undergoing growth pains and a change of philosophy.
In an apt turn of phrase, he called his demise "expansion
cracking." However, the internecine warfare turned out
much better than feared. Brower left the Club and similar
organizations reawakened to John Muir's principles.
Three months later, armed with his old enthusiasm and a
personal grant of $80,000 from the board chairman of
Atlantic Richfield, he announced creation of the educational John Muir Institute. More importantly, he founded
Friends of the Earth, a citizens' group that has cooperated
with the Sierra Club while outstripping the Club's renewed activism.

Garrett Hardin. University of California.

Chapter 14

Garrett Hardin and Overpopulation: Lifeboats vs. Mountain Climbers

Turn round the wagons here.

— Louis Simpson

He sits contendedly sawing away on his violin with another scientist and two philosophers of the *Salsi Puedas* (get out if you can) Quartet. In this setting the amateur music lover seems innocent enough. "He wears a string tie," comments Ralph Miller, a young journalist expecting other than the benign veneer, "and sports coat with a tiny gold pin in the lapel, a circle-and-arrow that looks like a Volvo ad but is really some sort of ecology symbol. If it were a Masonic pin instead, you'd take him immediately for a tourist from Kalamazoo...."

In fact, the inconspicuous ornament is a vasectomy pin, a reproduction of the male symbol used by biologists, but with a slice missing from the circle. It is a quiet reminder of the professor's career as an iconoclast. The images he is helping to break are many, the sacred cows that Western civilization worships. In the process he manages to pique racial minorities, sociologists, churchmen, political liberals and conservatives alike. In earlier times he might have ended his days tied and burning at a stake. As it is, Norman Counsins scourged the Santa Barbara professor from the editorial pages of the *Saturday Review*: "Hardinism can become a wild infection in the moral consciousness." Cousins was reacting to attacks on the shibboleths of Western society: freedom, philanthropy, technology. In the Hardin view, overpopulation and freedom are mutually exclusive. A surplus population degrades the environment, depriving individuals of a quality life. Besides this, as populations grow they become more complex, requiring restrictions on political rights. In Hardin's words, "Democracy is impossible with large numbers because the communication load goes up as the square of the population size."

Considering the environmental awareness of the mid-twentieth century, there is little shocking in the view itself. What stirs opposition is the difficult changes Hardin sees as necessary for society. People no longer should have the right to raise as many children as they wish because "loss of freedom to breed is less horrible than massive death by starvation, epidemics, social chaos, and insanity." In other words, society must yield one freedom in order to protect the others.

If this observation displeases some groups, other Hardin stances inflame them. Current welfare practices are absurd because they don't link rights with responsibilities: "In a welfare state everybody pays part of the cost of unwanted children," children who place demands on an already overburdened environment. Sensible people limit their families, notes Hardin as he presses the argument, yet they are forced to subsidize the ecological mistakes of the fast breeders. He looks with genuine sorrow on the starving poor of the world but concludes that their plight is hopeless. As to technology, people have persuaded themselves that it will save them from the ecological sin of overpopulation. Such agricultural innovations as the Green Revolution require huge amounts of capital, fertilizer, and machinery, while ignoring the fundamental problems of too many mouths and declining resources. The Santa Barbara professor shows statistically that the present population explosion is an historical perversion, a cancer. He irks some humanitarians by warning, "You can't cure a cancer by feeding it."

Personally good-natured, Hardin couches the urgency of his message in witty statements and cunning metaphors. The mutually antagonistic rantings of superconservatives and leftists are silly, because in practice the two systems they advocate overlap: "Every time John Birch sits down on the toilet, he becomes a socialist." Further, both political beliefs are environmental negatives, since they promote growth at the expense of a limited earth. His basic metaphor for current world problems — whether they be overpopulation or pesticide pollution — is the commons, a public pasture once shared by stockmen in England and in some parts of the American colonies. In his essay "The Tragedy of the Commons," he explains that the commons system will work, but only as long as the number of cattle does not exceed the carrying capacity. If a farmer increases his herd — which he is likely to do, given human greed — his quick gain means loss to others in the eventual overgrazing of the pasture. In other words, "Freedom in a commons brings ruin to all." The earth's soil, minerals, water, and air make up one vast but exploited commons. Calls for voluntary restraint, however morally appealing, are ridiculous. Those with consciences play the fool, outbred and outpolluted, as the case may be, by the conscienceless. The only hope is regulation by law, "mutual coercion, mutually agreed upon."

However, as Gifford Pinchot found when he brought regulation to the National Forests, it is a lesson that goes down hard in the United States, a nation with a history of chaotic settlement. There, quips Hardin, the modus operandi was to live "like gorillas: make a new nest every night, crap all over everything, then move on."

Behind Hardin's middle-aged celebrity lies a somewhat plodding if satisfying academic career. He was born in Dallas, Texas, but his father's clerical job with the Illinois Central Railroad required frequent moves throughout the Midwest. Polio crippled the boy in 1919 at the age of four. Still, the youth became an expert swimmer, and after high school in Chicago he considered becoming an actor — a career he abandoned because his shortened right leg would limit his stage roles. Instead, perhaps remembering pleasant summers spent on his grandfather's farm in Missouri, he majored in zoology at the University of Chicago, then went on to receive his Ph.D. in biology from Stanford in 1941. Five years later he gave up research on producing food from algae — an early sign of his intellectual independence. More food, he reasoned, only worsens the world's population problems. Regardless of the stance, his activism lay far in the future. The next fifteen years were spent upgrading the biology offerings at the University of California's Santa Barbara campus. Hardin made educational films, introduced closed circuit television to the classroom, and wrote a widely-used text, *Biology: Its Human Implications* (1949). A 1959 book, *Nature and Man's Fate,* deals with the social consequences of evolution. Along with a course in human ecology he developed a year later, it shows a shift in the biologist's concerns.

The rebirth of conservation — and the accelerated social changes that are its matrix — began after World War II and came to fruition in the 1960's. Hardin chides himself for not coming to his ecological conclusions earlier. A tongue-in-cheek Hardin formula explains his slow development: *"It takes five years for a person's mind to change."* In his case it took a succession of five-year changes that paralleled the general environmental awareness growing across the nation. He became an activist at a time when ideas were ripe for the picking, to use his own cliché. Yet there were dangers.

Contrary to one public myth, universities are not entirely bastions of sweetness and light. Despite their high purposes, day-to-day operations are just as susceptible to outside politics and internal squabbles as are those of other institutions. With others of his generation, Hardin had labored through the Depression to his Ph.D. in anticipation of a relatively secure teaching position. Over the years, he had served Santa Barbara, a small liberal arts college when he joined the faculty, well. After the War, however, college enrollment soared. Ambitious college presidents, their eyes on burgeoning expenses, changed the rules. Education became big business, now emphasizing success in money-generating research rather than in the less measurable fruits of successful teaching. In the meantime, Hardin had quit laboratory work entirely, saying, "I saw no signs that I had any great talent as a laboratory researcher." Instead he turned his energies to popularizing science among his students and with the general public. Not that he was in immediate danger of losing his job. The tenure system offered some protection, barring an academic conviction of malfeasance. Then, too, by this time his worthy though unglamorous teaching accomplishments had been rewarded by his rise to the highest pedagogical rank, a full professorship. Still, America was just emerging from the McCarthy era. Censorship, though not openly condoned, was practiced. In recounting his environmental emergence in *Stalking the Wild Taboo* (1973), Hardin asks for a leap backward in the imagination: "It is essential that the reader recognize that abortion was a strongly tabooed topic in 1963. So much has the world changed in the past decade that this recognition takes a bit of imagination, but you can't understand history without imagination. Most newspapers in 1963 would not print the word 'abortion'; even those that would avoided the subject if they could. It was no light matter for a professor in a state university — my situation — to take a public position against the prohibition of abortion."

Yet that's what he did. When the faculty invited him to give a university-wide lecture on a subject of current interest to him, he chose the topic of population control through legalized abortion. Noting the public's reluctance to examine taboos, a fellow academician has dubbed Garrett Hardin "one psychologically brave, but professionally foolish soul."

During the 1960's California "discovered the Frisbee, embraced vodka and popularized credit cards," as *Time* magazine puts it. The state also was the crucible of deeper intellectual changes. Despite his fears "hate mail and vituperative phone calls" didn't materialize after the speech. Instead, the audience honored him with intense questions, both pro and con. He was especially impressed, however, during the following days, when "eminently respectable women" congratulated him on the street and told him about their own secret abortions. Apparently, abortion was a reality that the public chose to ignore. He started digging into history books to ferret out the story of the earth's population.

He found that for thousands of years disease, starvation, abortion, and widespread infanticide had kept the earth's population relatively stable, with a yearly average increase of 0.032 percent. Though people tend to accept present situations as normal for all times, the current two-percent growth rate, seen in the perspective of history, is abnormal. It would have people occupying every square foot of land in a mere 615 years. Hardin's population articles joined *Famine–1975!* (1967) by William and

"Freedom in a commons brings ruin to all," according to Hardin.
*"Those with consciences play the fool, outbred and outpolluted by
the conscienceless."* High Country News.

Paul Paddock and *The Population Bomb* (1968) by Paul Ehrlich in warning that the world had overburdened its life-support systems. Mass starvation already had started in India and Africa. Yet he had a further step to take: what is to be done about the situation? His positions often make Hardin seem callous to suffering, though he counters the charge with the maxim "we can never do nothing." Either we take fate into our own hands, or our lack of action will increase suffering when nature solves the population problems by its own means — as it has done heartlessly time after time in the past.

If his view of abortion that "smashing acorns is not deforestation, scrambling eggs is not gallicide" offended right-to-life groups and some religious leaders, his next proposal brought some fellow scientists who had supported him to their feet in rage. Appearing in the October 1974 issue of *BioScience*, "Living on a Lifeboat" proposed a solution through another Hardin metaphor.

Hardin is a wide-ranging reader, an asset for the generalist. He quotes George Eliot, George Bernard Shaw, and W.S. Gilbert with ease in backing up his arguments. The earlier "Tragedy of the Commons" owed its inspiration to a tract by an obscure nineteenth-century amateur mathematician, William Forster Lloyd. For "Life on a Lifeboat" the biologist drew on an unusual bit of naval history. In the last century the *William Brown* sank. Survivors clung to a single wooden boat, so overloaded that it in turn threatened to founder. In order to keep the craft afloat, leaders ordered a number of the passengers killed. Though morally irreconcilable, the immediate choices were clear: either some must be sacrificed or all would drown. The *BioScience* essay likened the environmentally overburdened world to the plight of the shipwrecked: "Metaphorically, each rich nation amounts to a lifeboat full of comparatively rich people. The poor of the world are in other, much more crowded lifeboats. Continuously, so to speak, the poor fall out of their lifeboats and swim for a while in the water outside, hoping to be admitted to a rich lifeboat, or in some other way to benefit from the 'goodies' on board. What should the passengers on a rich lifeboat do?"

Given the metaphor, the answer is painful but inescapable. The people in the rich lifeboats must abandon the poor in order to save themselves. Otherwise no one will survive. Hardin analyzed the list of possibilities for helping the earth's overpopulated countries: technology, world food banks, immigration. Each draws on the limited resources of the rich, causing more suffering in the long run and resulting in everyone's demise. The lifeboat, like all ecological systems, is a finite commons. Hardin admitted that the solution was unfair to the victims, but he reminded readers that, whatever their sentiments, survival in nature is not based on a human system of justice.

In the next few months, letters and articles hotly disputing his thesis appeared in popular magazines and scientific journals. Norman Cousins railed from two editorials in the *Saturday Review* against "the notion that some people have the right to decide whether others should live or die" — ignoring the fact that the United States already is forced to do so in allocating its limited surplus food. Others attacked the metaphor with greater skill. In the May 1975 issue of *BioScience,* members of the Hudson River Ecological Survey compared the world's nations to mountain climbers connected by safety ropes. The survival of the group depends on the survival of each climber. Critical mineral and oil deposits held by third-world powers, plus the proliferation of nuclear weapons, make cooperation, rather than exclusion, a necessity in the interconnected world, they maintained. Over the years a similar argument has been put forth by Hardin critics such as biologist Barry Commoner, who maintains that misused technology rather than overpopulation is primarily responsible for critical strains on the world's resources.

Whatever the detractions, Garrett Hardin continues to plunge on, often jovially, ahead of his critics. *Exploring New Ethics for Survival: The Voyage of the Spaceship* Beagle (1972) illustrates, by a take off on science fiction, what he sees as new moral dictates. In the future setting of the story, advocates of growth have "tired of the apocalyptic rantings of Paul Ehrlich" and castrated Garrett Hardin "with a dull aluminum spoon." However, growth mania has run its course; confronted with an uninhabitable planet, earthlings send a sample of their kind off in search of a home in space. Unfortunately, they must take along with them their all too-human frailties.

Stalking the Wild Taboo (1973) echoes Freudian psychology while debunking popular myths. It maintains that Western society, with its faith in technology, is motivated by its own set of superstitions. It believes that quantity is better than quality, that knowledge is better than ignorance, that science can solve human problems. Hardin suggests that the space program is a form of fantasy, an escape from earthly realities orchestrated by the modern equivalents of witch doctors. He chastizes sociologists and biologists, two tribes disputing overlapping territories. In the Hardin view, society cannot insure its environmental future until it comes to terms with such prejudices.

It is difficult to say how literally Hardin intends his metaphors or how seriously he takes his own arguments. However, he has succeeded if his purpose is nothing more than to push critical situations into the forefront of controversy. In the words of population expert Paul Ehrlich, "whether I agree with the lifeboat ethics argument or not is secondary to the fact that it was very important that he put it forth. I am not so confident of my views to say that I'm right and Garrett's wrong. I tend to disagree with him on that, but Garrett's a very smart guy and I think the best

writer among living biologists." Along with other conservationists, Garrett Hardin has been attacked for reminding the public of ecological necessities. He has shared the
epithet of insensitive elitist. In John McPhee's *Encounters
with the Archdruid,* David Brower explains that deep
human concerns for the future are the bases for Hardin's
controversial theories. Referring to the destructive impact of a growing population on the nation's limited and
fragile wilderness heritage, Brower notes: "I have a friend
named Garrett Hardin, who wears leg braces. I have
heard him say that he would not want to be able to come to
a place like this by road, and that it is enough for him just
to know that these mountains exist as they are, and he
hopes that they will be like this in the future."

Stewart Udall. Stewart Udall.

Chapter 15

Working from Within:
Stewart Udall Finds Conservation
Good Politics

"...the bonfire
you kindle can light the great sky –
though it's true, of course, to make it burn
you have to throw yourself in...."

— Galway Kinnell

In 1880 the Mormon Church made David King Udall a bishop and sent him off to shore up a struggling colony in the Arizona wilderness. Dutifully he loaded two wagons and started out from Kanab, Utah, with his young wife Ella, who a decade earlier had sent out news over the Church's telegraph system of John Wesley Powell's Southwest explorations. After a month and four hundred miles, David Udall arrived to take charge of a few Mormon families clustered on the banks of the Little Colorado River and establish the town of St. Johns. He found the soil poor, the weather on the high Colorado Plateau tending toward blizzards and droughts. Worse, non-Mormons in the sparsely settled area welcomed the newcomers by tearing down their fences. Near riots occurred. A court

173

convicted Bishop Udall on trumped-up perjury charges
and shipped him off to a Detroit jail. Granted a pardon by
President Cleveland, the bishop returned to hold his colony together.

The town never prospered in any modern sense. Today
the farming community is about the same size as it was at
the turn of the century. But in the few generations since
St. Johns' frontier days, the Udall family has branched out
into law, politics, and business, becoming one of the most
powerful in the state. Two grandchildren of David Udall
have gained national attention. Congressman Morris
Udall came close to winning the Democratic nomination
for the 1976 Presidential election. He remains the lone
progressive, conservation-minded Representative from a
politically conservative and environmentally listless
state.

His brother Stewart Udall became Secretary of the Interior in 1961, at the age of forty-one among the youngest
to hold the post. He stayed in the office for eight years
under Presidents Kennedy and Johnson, a term second
only to that of Harold Ickes. Stewart Udall rivals Ickes in
other ways. In a burst of enthusiasm, prime mover of the
1964 Wilderness Act, Rep. John P. Saylor, praised Udall
as "the greatest secretary that has ever held the office."
Given the vicissitudes of history, such an honor is difficult
to certify, but Ickes' progressive performance marks a
high point for conservation by the government. Viewing
the Department of Interior as a many-armed instrument
of resource preservation, during the Depression he reflected the environmental concerns of President Franklin
Delano Roosevelt by thwarting special interests to expand
the National Park system. He supported passage of the
Taylor Grazing Act of 1934, which brought effective regulation of livestock on public lands, and helped stem the
loss of America's precious topsoil, blowing away during
the Dust Bowl.

For all that, generations to come will look upon Udall's work as exceptional, perhaps unequaled — a lesson in political survival combined with effective conservation. As he left office in 1969, the *New Republic* offered a panegyric:

> Udall... has left a legacy nobody can touch — six new national seashores, four national parks, two national recreation areas, the first national trail, and the first national system of wild and scenic rivers. Interior set up a Bureau of Outdoor Recreation in 1962; fought for Congressional funding of a Land and Water Conservation Fund in 1964....; and broke a ten-year deadlock in Congress to establish a National Wilderness Preservation System.

The praise reflects only the surface of accomplishments. For instance, the concept underlying the Wilderness System took hold at least as far back as 1924, when Aldo Leopold persuaded the Forest Service to set aside one-half million wild acres in New Mexico as a preserve. Udall's political maneuverings helped bring forty years of conservation struggle to fruition.

The Udall legacy shines according to any standards, but it takes on a near solar brightness when seen in the light of the Department's long-term performance, a one-hundred-and-thirty year history marked by wild seesawing between profligacy and preservation. President Zachary Taylor established the Department of Interior in 1849. Its first bureau was the General Land Office, which winked at its own giveaways of the public's domain to railroads, lumber companies, and corporate land speculators. Gifford Pinchot, Chief of the Forest Service in the rival Department of Agriculture, looked across Washington with a bilious eye on what he saw as Interior's come-and-get-it attitudes toward resources, and since then the Department has remained suspect in con-

servationists' eyes. Certainly the wealth of Interior's holdings and the variety of its functions make it a natural for
the spoils system, a "sluiceway" for corruption, in Senator
Robert LaFollette's view. Today the Department controls
about one-fourth of the nation's land area — most of it in
the West. Its Secretary has wide latitude in shaping the
future of the National Park Service, the Bureau of Land
Management, the Fish and Wildlife Service, and the lives
of a half million Indians, to mention a few of his functions.
He is responsible for mineral, oil, forest, and water resources — some of the richest prizes in the country but also
traditional targets for exploitation.

Some Secretaries, notably Carl Schurz, John W. Noble,
Hoke Smith, James R. Garfield, Franklin K. Lane, and
John Payne, deserve ranking with the country's heroes.
Along with Ickes and Udall, they not only resisted the
temptation of easy gains for themselves and friends but
defended the public's land — frequently amid public out-
cries of government interference. They were the exceptions, and often these men owed their successes as much to
sympathetic Presidents backed by sometimes rambunc-
tious conservationists as to indivdual altruism and
foresight.

On the other extreme stand men like Richard A.
Ballinger, Pinchot's archenemy during the Taft Administration, and Albert Bacon Fall. When Fall swag-
gered into Interior's offices at the beginning of the Harding era, the artifacts courteously left by previous Secretaries delighted him. He ordered the treasures packed
up and sent to his ranch in New Mexico. The longer he
stayed in office, the more grandiose became his ideas. He
drew up blueprints placing his ranch at the center of a new
National Park, one open to mining, hunting, and lumber-
ing. Congress wisely shrugged off the proposal. Today, he
is better known for sub-rosa gratuities received from oil
companies. Fall's greedy career ended when these bribes

A former farmboy and B-24 gunner, Udall added fifty-nine areas to the National Park system and resisted developments in others. "Posterity will honor us more for the roads and dams we do not build than for those we do," he said. His zealousness for preservation shocked folks back home in St. Johns, Arizona. U.S. Department of Interior.

blossomed into the Teapot Dome scandal of the 1920's.

Udall's immediate predecessor, Fred A. Seaton, advocated park expansion and the protection of wildlife refuges but also shared the Administration's attitude toward spending nature's capital. More dramatic was the first Eisenhower appointee, an automobile dealer from Salem, Oregon. While millions of people swarmed over the National Parks during a period of unprecedented use, Douglas McKay pontificated that he saw no need for park expansion. He called conservationists "punks." The election of John F. Kennedy presaged a more sympathetic approach toward the earth. Whatever the final assessment of Kennedy's Administration, never before had a President asked a poet — and one inspired by his own love for and struggles with the American soil — to bless his inauguration. As the aging but cagey Robert Frost read the line, "The land was ours before we were the land's," conservationists felt the coming change. Kennedy's choice of cabinet officers reflected youthful hope and enlightened buoyancy. In surveying the new roster, a national magazine described the typical appointee as "bright, tough-minded, hard-working and athletic."

Udall, a former farmboy, B-24 gunner, athlete, and Congressman from Arizona's backwoods, matched the Kennedy image as well as that of the ambitious Udall family. After missionary work for the Mormon Church and flying service in Italy during World War II, Stewart Udall starred on the University of Arizona's first championship basketball team. He received his law degree in 1948, opened a practice in Tucson, then served three terms in Washington as Representative from the Second District, which at the time covered the entire state, minus its capital, Phoenix.

In Congress he worked for civil rights and labor reform and sat on the Committee on Interior and Insular Affairs. Eyebrows in rural St. Johns went up at his liberal drift, but he kept political fences mended back home: Arizona's Second District benefited from more federal money than any other Congressman's. More important to Udall's future, then-Senator John F. Kennedy took note of the Arizonan's help in passing Kennedy-favored labor legislation. Udall's prospects for higher office brightened in 1960. By deft maneuvering during the Democratic National Convention, he delivered his state's seventeen votes, thought assured for Lyndon Johnson, to the Massachusetts senator. The Secretaryship of Interior was his reward.

Well over six-feet tall, lean, and crewcut, Udall came

bouncing into Interior determined to turn the former "sluiceway" into the "department of the future." He reminded reporters of the Udall tradition of public service. "It came from my father. Maybe he didn't make much money at it," intoned the Secretary, "but he instilled in us kids the belief that if we were fit for such service we should not avoid it." That made folksy newspaper copy, and his style moved critics, among them former Vice-President Richard Nixon, to snarl at Udall's "cheap and vicious" performances. Udall heated his Washington home with firewood, keeping it a brisk 55° in winter, and led puffing Congressmen on expeditions to sites for future National Parks. In the field, he delighted photographers by leaping fences. On one occasion a Udall party helicoptered onto the prospective Grasslands National Park, only to be ordered back into the air by an irate Kansas rancher. The Secretary wouldn't leave, however, until the rancher agreed to shake hands—while Associated Press cameras recorded Udall's good sportsmanship.

Yet, as was true of Stephen Mather's similar methods, there was substance behind Udall's style. By the end of 1961, Interior had added eleven National Wildlife Refuges and Ranges to its domain. In response to population pressures that were locking out the public from its coastline, the Department initiated a system of National Seashores, the first substantial enlargements of the National Parks in fourteen years. The Secretary then announced his main goal: to place 15-20 million acres — acres that he called "human life refuges" — under park care. Perhaps President Kennedy was more concerned with the progressive image of his Administration than for the details of Interior's new life. Whatever the case, the President gave Udall his lead. By putting in sixteen-hour days, Udall wrote *The Quiet Crisis* (1963), a land history of the United States, which shows the tutelage of novelist Wallace Stegner, briefly a member of the Udall staff. The

Secretary topped the accomplishment by persuading Kennedy to contribute the introduction: "We must do in our day what Theodore Roosevelt did sixty years ago and Franklin Roosevelt did thirty years ago...." It was a strong endorsement of Interior's aggressive policies.

When Lyndon Johnson stepped into the Presidency after the Kennedy assassination, politicos remembered Udall's crucial swing of Arizona delegates three years earlier and predicted the Secretary's departure. However, the new President recognized the value of highly visible programs in aggrandizing his own large schemes for the Great Society. Udall not only stayed but received more active support from the White House than he had under Kennedy. As one Interior official interpreted the situation, "Conservation now has become a big political issue, and worth capitalizing on."

Udall had already shown his willingness to get down to "brass tacks," as an editorial in *American Forests* assessed his work, by making basic policy changes. In an overdue move to stop deterioration of the public domain, Interior had doubled the grazing fees on Bureau of Land Management ranges, an action long resisted by the powerful grazing lobby. Now, with Johnson's support, he launched another expansion of the parks on a scale not seen since New Deal days. By the end of his administration, he had added fifty-nine areas to the National Park System. All the while, he indulged Mrs. Johnson, who had her own pet beautification projects, by shooting down the Colorado rapids with her. Meanwhile, he followed the examples of John Muir and Enos Mills, and promoted his own performance as Secretary of Interior, with a colorful format book, *The National Parks of America* (1966).

While he publicized his activities, his outlook deepened. Following the environmental trend, he espoused a more holistic approach to nature, and he envisioned himself a leader of the "new conservation," a movement concerned with the total environment: "...you can't isolate anything any more.... You plan for what things are going to be like 50 years from now...." He put forth a comprehensive plan for the future in *1976: Agenda for Tomorrow* (1968). The book linked environmental gains to broad social changes: "You cannot, in short, save the land unless you save the people." The views further jolted folks back in St. Johns — always hopeful for the quick salvation of development — when summed up in such unmistakable thrusts as, "...posterity will honor us more for the roads and dams we do not build... than those we do." Whatever they owed to current clichés, Udall's sweeping prospects marked a departure for a Secretary of Interior.

Udall was among the first high government officials to defend the conclusions of Rachel Carson's *Silent Spring*. However, political historians have not yet made comprehensive evaluations of Stewart Udall's heady years in government. One might suggest they will find he was an expert politician with a strong conservation bent, though the leanings were not often allowed to endanger his political career — perhaps the very reason for his environmental successes. A case in point is the controversy in the 1960's over plugging the Grand Canyon with Marble and Bridge Canyon Dams. Since the 1940's, Arizonans had looked on the Central Arizona Project as a future answer to their water problems. No politician of any note in the state had survived without blessing the surrealistic system of pumping stations, dams, and aqueducts that would bring water from the already overdrawn Colorado River to fill swimming pools in suburban Phoenix and make the state's deserts bloom with surplus cotton. For years the political climate forced Udall to support the complex. However, aroused by David Brower and others, conservationists across the nation rallied fiercely when time came to build the dams. The movement gave the Secretary of Interior the needed political base for a shift in the government's position. In 1967, while Arizonans gasped, he recommended against the two dams and persuaded President Johnson to designate Marble Canyon a national monument.

In 1968 the National Audubon Society conferred official recognition on Udall with its yearly Audubon Medal, a laurel shared in the past by such environmental pillars as Rachel Carson, William O. Douglas, and Olaus Murie. While the end of his term neared, Mr. Johnson fairly glowed in his reputation, earned primarily by Udall, as a conservation President. Meanwhile, as Mr. Nixon prepared to take office, both Johnson and Udall eyed Walter Hickel, the incoming Interior Secretary. He had publicly blustered: "Just to withdraw a large area for conservation purposes and lock it up for no reason doesn't have any merit in my opinion." The two lame ducks laid plans to bring off a final coup to confirm their reputations in conservation's history books. Echoing creation of the "midnight forests" by Teddy Roosevelt and Pinchot, they planned to add 7.5 million last-minute acres to the park system by using the executive option under the Antiquities Act of 1906. Mr. Johnson expansively announced the gift to the nation on television, and Interior rushed out the details in a press release. But in the following days the plan soured. Congressmen murmured that the President had left them out of the scheme. For his part, in a last burst of enthusiasm Udall irked Johnson by planning to rename the District of Columbia Stadium after a Johnson rival, the late Robert Kennedy. In a fulminating phone call the President told Udall the park addition was off. Udall shouted back his offer to resign. In last-minute pettiness the nation lost a major expansion of its parks. Despite his overall record, Stewart Udall left office a disappointed man.

Whatever the role of political expediency, Stewart Udall continues to pursue the environmental goals he articulated when a government official. Articles in *National Wildlife* and the *Atlantic Monthly* have prodded subsequent administrations about the anachronistic mining law of 1872 and the country's addiction to the automobile. He served on the board of directors of the National Wildlife Federation, moderated the series "Issues in the Environmental Crisis" at Yale University, and wrote a syndicated newspaper column, "Our Environment." As chairman of the Overview Group, an international consulting firm, he advised industries and governments on long-range environmental planning. In the spirit of John Wesley Powell's *Arid Lands, The Energy Balloon* (1974) demythologized popular assumptions and set forth rational alternatives to debilitating growth. Currently Stewart Udall works as a hired gun for environmental groups, advocating open space, opposing freeways, and giving advice on energy problems wherever his legal skills can be of help.

Edward Abbey. Bruce Hamilton.

Chapter 16

Working from Without: Edward Abbey, Part Zorro, Part Ezekiel

> *Be true, be true*
> *to your own strange kind.*
>
> — Louis Simpson

Wielding oversized golden scissors, the governors of Utah and Arizona strut to the middle of a new bridge spanning the Colorado River. After the standard flatulent speeches, they bend to cut the ceremonial ribbon. To their amazement rockets and bombs shoot into the air, the bridge leaps skyward, then collapses into the gorge below, leaving only limp tie rods dangling from the bedrock at either end. Moments later a plume of smoke, like a giant exclamation point, rises out of the chasm. The opening scene of Edward Abbey's *The Monkey Wrench Gang* (1975) is a mere preview of the exploits of a kooky but idealistic band. At night the eco-raiders, "warped but warped in the right way," sally forth from Utah's canyons to defend the fragile land in an orgy of guerrilla warfare against what they see as the industrialized madness — the new strip mines, power plants, and highways — that is destroying it.

"I'm a humanist," its author explains elsewhere in his typically sardonic vein. "I'd rather kill a man than a snake." The statement arises from the major concerns of his writing, the appreciation of natural beauty and anger at its needless loss, which have fueled ten books and more than twenty articles. Conservation literature of the past is full of praises of nature's beauty; anger, when it appears, usually is designed to move readers to the gentlemanly pursuits of writing Congressmen, certainly no more than parading with signs displaying harmless slogans. So it is that in the public mind Abbey's full-blown rage is what distinguishes him from others. "What's more American than violence?" asks the demolitions expert of the raiders. A veteran of the Vietnam War and Army mental institutions, the Abbey character remembers napalm and defoliants broadcast over helpless peasants and rich farmlands. To him the gouging of the earth taking place in his own country is simply the warfare of a mindless military-industrial complex applied to American soil.

"I consider myself a savage, vicious, embittered, utterly irresponsible critic of our society and for years, in my writing, I have been cultivating the art of the arrogant sneer, the venomous put-down, the elegant hatchet job. I want to be feared; I want to be hated," Abbey rails against developers of the Rocky Mountains, which like Enos Mills he considers his own territory, an extension of his personality. Abbey's cataclysmic vision is of a world gone mad with technology, racing toward catastrophe. Reflecting the frustrations of other movements over the recent past, Abbey urges anarchy as the only effective response: the dynamiting of dams, the surreptitious pouring of Karo syrup into the vitals of bulldozers. The view would have appalled gentle John Muir, who, in a different time, had faith in rational solutions. And in the minds of the apostles of growth, this view discredits Abbey as another "irresponsible, subversive wilderness nut." Conservationists, with their favorable public image and tradition of applying steady pressure from within the political framework, might chuckle at Abbey's antics as naughty wish fulfillment. In public, however, almost all of them have stood clear of Abbey's frenetic brand of anarchism, letting him take the brunt of counterattacks. That is fine with Ed Abbey, who proclaims that his most admired animal is the crocodile, that he will return in a future life as a soaring vulture — that, anyhow, he is too ignorant and lazy to be a conservationist.

To what extent is this sulfurous writer a poseur? Like Mary Austin, he has chosen to earn a living from his pen, no easy task in twentieth-century America. Again as with Austin, and to a lesser degree Muir, a certain manufactured public image — in his case of a snide, often flippant Ezekiel — has helped sell books and fill lecture halls to overflowing. With other contemporary writers, Abbey enjoys the put-on, delights in pulling the public's leg, revels in the shock value of the pyromaniacal anarchists darting through the shadows of his novels. Frequently it isn't clear where Abbey the disgruntled idealist ends and Abbey the leg-pulling mischief begins. It may be that Abbey himself doesn't know — and doesn't care. His politics add to the confusion. Conservation generally is associated with broader liberal causes, as reflected in the lives of Pinchot, Austin, and William O. Douglas. Often exploitation of nature finds its strongest support among conservatives. Abbey's stance has a foot in each camp. His advocacy of private ownership of firearms as defense against tyranny and his wish for the least government possible might draw applause from the political right — if it weren't for his equally vehement condemnation of industrial growth and of the corporate America that promotes it.

Yet Abbey doesn't care about consistent political views. All he wants is the old American dream, to be left alone in the wilderness, which he associates with wildness, freedom, fulfillment. To him the wilderness is the one spiritual underpinning that can define his life, bring peace and consistency in a chaotic, self-destructive world. From boyhood his has been a wildly fluctuating search for the romantic ideal reflected in his books, an ideal he has found corroding in the West's deserts and mountains, an ideal which much of America has yearned to find there. The fact that the industrialized outside world is making war on his refuge has pushed him, according to his own lights, to the forefront of defending what he loves — not for society's sake — but for his own.

Whatever calculated froth might accompany them, both his anger and painful sensitivity to beauty are genuine. He is the daring romantic hero — a figure with appeal to a good part of the public. Chafing from the strictures of industrialization and overpopulation, this public not only recognizes the practical necessity of conservation, it also longs for a taste — even a vicarious taste — of its fast fading wilderness heritage. As a result, his books have encouraged legions of movers and shakers who somewhat more passively share his concerns. In the words of *Publishers Weekly,* the Utahan has become "one of the most outspoken and eloquent exponents of an environmental viewpoint." And his occasional mocking of environmental groups to the contrary, he has set an example, giving generously of his time and often lean finances to support the cause that lies at the heart of his writing — the preservation of wild America.

One of his pithy self-observations explains, "I put the best part of me in my books; the evil side I hope to keep secret." That might further a writer's romantic image with his audience, but it is not entirely true of Edward

Abbey. In fact, with some variation, the author's life is the subject of his books. In the best romantic tradition, Abbey the writer and Abbey the man are much the same person. Craggy-faced, lean, cagey in private conversation, he is the image of the desert rat with a shady past projected by the heroes of his novels. Whether or not he carries out the militant tactics recommended in his books, an edgy power surrounds Ed Abbey the man, potential violence set on hair trigger. He tells admirers gauche enough to ask that he lives in Wolf Hole, Arizona, a place that, mostly, doesn't exist. That false trail is a calculated part of his literary mystique. It is also a form of self-protection for a writer who must put bread on the table by dint of his production, but who finds himself the target of overweening enthusiasts. Actually he lives on the outskirts of one of the isolated Mormon hamlets tucked away in the rocky folds of the Colorado Plateau. It is a refuge that he gained by a circuitous route. No doubt literature professors will make much of the writer's archetypically American sense of rootlessness, his Adamic agonies and ecstasies in finding a home — and with a good deal of justification, though to the chagrin of Edward Abbey, a detractor of long-faced academe.

Though Travernian mists float over some of his past, its general outlines are not obscure. He was born in 1927 on a farm near Home, Pennsylvania — and Abbey has not let the irony in the place-name pass: "I found myself a displaced person shortly after birth and have been looking half my life for a place to take my stand." Like many an Abbey statement, it consists of truth mixed with exaggeration. His childhood, though materially poor, had an idyllic quality of the pristine to it. Abbey's grandfather was from a village in Switzerland, and Edward's father, continuing the rural tradition as "a logger, sawyer, and woodsman," made his home in the lesser, though richly wooded, mountains of the northern Appalachians. With his two brothers, young Abbey helped with the standard farm chores. But the boys enjoyed plenty of freedom:

> Vines of wild grape trailed from the limbs of ancient druidical oaks — dark glens of mystery and shamanism. My brothers and I, simple-minded farmboys, knew nothing of such mythologies, but we were aware, all the same, of the magic residing among and within those trees. We knew that the Indians had once been here, Seneca and Shawnee, following the same deer paths.... We knew all about moccasins and feathers, arrows and bows, the thrill of sneaking naked through the underbrush, taking care to tread on not a single dry twig. Our lore came from boys' books, but it was the forest that made it real.

The sense of beauty and mystery was also the beginning of pain. In the accelerated development after World War II, Abbey would witness the assault on a natural world that once had lent wonder, meaning, and security to his life.

For the meantime the farmboy was afflicted with wanderlust. In 1944, having grown up through the Depression, at the age of seventeen, baby-faced and naive, he set out on a hitchhiking tour to see the West — a land important to much of America's youthful dreams — before the Army could thrust him into the holocaust then going on in Europe and the Pacific. And as for so many other Americans over the generations, that journeying West marked a coming of age, a self-discovery. *The Journey Home* (1977) tells of his first glimpse of the distant Rockies, "an impossible beauty, like a boy's first sight of an undressed girl," of his involvement in a robbery that has a light-hearted Huck Finn ring to it, of his horror at first seeing humans turned into robots on a production line. For all that, what most impressed him and changed his life was his view from the door of a swaying boxcar of the Southwest's mountains and deserts. Much would intervene in a long scrambled period of settling down before he returned there permanently to make what he refers to in his half serious, half self-chiding way as "Abbey's last stand."

In 1945 the Army sent him to Italy, from which the infantryman returned two years later, still a private, a rebel against authority in general and organized activities in particular. The pain of it was that Abbey also was drawn to success in more traditional ways — a tension that adds complexity to his life and writing. Otherwise, he might have ended up as just another disgruntled desert rat. Using the University of New Mexico as a home base, he took ten years of study interspersed with ramblings to earn an undergraduate degree and then an M.A. in philosophy. The duality of his personality is reflected by the fact that the budding extremist suffered through the discipline of writing a master's thesis entitled *Anarchism and the Morality of Violence.* He also exercised his rebellious glee while editing *The Thunderbird,* a student literary publication. In his monograph *Edward Abbey,* Garth McCann reports: "His editorship exploded suddenly in the furor surrounding the March 1951 issue which contained his own story, 'Some Implications of Anarchy,' and the following epigram from Voltaire, which he ironically ascribed to Louisa May Alcott and which appeared on the cover: 'Man will never be free until the last king is strangled with the entrails of the last priest.' By the time the local religious and civil authorities had finished roasting that *Thunderbird,* most of the copies had been seized and the magazine staff and supporters were temporarily in serious trouble."

Yet the former editor not only survived, he did it with a certain élan. Abbey the Searcher, torn between wholesale freedom and the strictures of academe, scurried back and forth between desert Albuquerque and the world outside, enjoying a Fulbright scholarship to Scotland at the University of Edinburgh, showing up in Wallace Stegner's creative writing class at Stanford, spending a mere two weeks at Yale working on his Ph.D. In the meantime, Dodd, Mead published his first book, *Jonathan Troy* (1954), a novel "about an intense and frustrated romanticist who lives in a Pennsylvania mining town," which the reviewer for the *New York Times* went on to summarize as "a symphony of disgust." The young writer had begun his career where, according to Goethe, romanticism ends: in morbidity. Fortunately, Abbey had the strength and vision not to stop in the sinkhole of self-pity. The second novel, *The Brave Cowboy* (1956), juxtaposes a Lone-Ranger style cowboy and the modern West. With its irony, adventure, wish fulfillment, its love of poking fun despite the sense of loss, its independent hero set against an overwhelming technology, the book established the themes for later novels, *Fire on the Mountain* (1962) and *Black Sun* (1971), as well as for the other writings that came as Abbey mused more deeply on his adopted home territory.

Yet as was true of the milder David Brower at a similar stage of his life, Abbey had not yet sunk his roots, had not yet ended his period of Sturm und Drang. Several times he returned to work in the industrialized East; each time he left in frustration for the less crowded West. In 1964 he moved to Hoboken, New Jersey. For a short while he produced training manuals for General Electric but was fired "for spending too much time staring out the window." He next took a job as a welfare worker in Brooklyn. Despite his love of the outdoors, Abbey was flexible in "Glitter Gulch, U.S.A." To a certain degree he could celebrate, as Walt Whitman did, the smell of the grease paint, "The blab of the pave...." Still, the West tugged at his imagination. After two years of Hoboken, he finally had enough of the rats that "raced in ferocious packs, like wolves," enough of his "happy little journey through hell." He escaped to a job as ranger at Organ Pipe Cactus Na-

Arches National Monument. In the Monkey Wrench Gang, *eco-
raiders sally forth from Utah's canyons to defend the fragile land
against new strip mines, power plants, and highways.* High Country News.

tional Monument, on the Arizona-Mexico border, where
he could contemplate the lonely desert sweeps.

As he approached the age of forty, Edward Abbey was
slowly circling in toward Wolf Hole to take his stand as an
advocate of wilderness. All the while he was writing books
and articles that show his increasing identification with
the land and his commitment to protect it. He also scrambled to support himself and a succession of four wives. *The
Brave Cowboy* was made into a movie, *Lonely Are the
Brave,* starring Kirk Douglas. That brought a little
money, $7,500, and if his other volumes made neither him
nor his publishers wealthy, living was cheap in Wolf Hole.
Winters he climbed peaks, roamed the deserts, and wrote;
summers provided more stable incomes. He spent them in
various places, working as a fire lookout and ranger at the
North Rim of the Grand Canyon, at Glacier National Park
in Montana, and in Utah's Arches National Monument.

Out of three summers at Arches came *Desert Solitaire: A Season in the Wilderness* (1968). It brought him his first substantial fame. Like many other works of the genre — Thoreau's *Walden,* Aldo Leopold's *A Sand County Almanac,* or Henry Beston's *The Outermost House* — it is a loosely-structured, reflective account of "days lingering and long, spacious and free as the summers of childhood," spent alone in the wilderness. What sets it off from other finely-drawn eulogies to nature, making the book a classic among backpackers and the larger number of armchair backpackers, is Abbey's outrage at the nation's assault on Arches National Monument and other last refuges of solitude and undeveloped landscapes. With the grim humor of the guerrilla who realizes his may well be a lost cause, Abbey shifts from sublime passages to stinging comments on tourists, whose first interest is the location of Coke machines, who dash madly through the country's National Parks in "motorized wheelchairs." The tourists, along with the highway builders and chambers of commerce, the motel chains and Congressmen and small-town mayors who are urging that the last patches of the wild West be turned into plasticized Disneylands, are participants in the nation's mass madness:"There are some who frankly and boldly advocate the eradication of the last remnants of wilderness and the complete subjugation of nature to the requirements of — not man — but industry. This is a courageous view, admirable in its simplicity and power, and with the weight of all modern history behind it. It is also quite insane."

In one scene the ranger's musings over browsing deer are interrupted by a jeep-load of beefy engineers. Their leader glows with the prospect of building a high-speed road through the undeveloped park, one that will bring twenty, perhaps thirty, times the visitors, who, overweight in their overweight cars, will gawk at the sculptured curiosities of Arches. "I knew that I was dealing with a madman," comments ranger Abbey. After they go grinding off over the landscape in their government vehicle, he spends the night in a futile but foreshadowing gesture of pulling up the survey stakes for their highway.

Desert Solitaire came at the right time. Four years earlier, Congress had passed the Wilderness Act. Enthusiasm for environmental reforms kept alive over the previous three or four decades by a small group of advocates was again taking hold in the public imagination. People were swelling the membership rolls of environmental groups, flocking into backpacking outlets for topographic maps, for the Vasque boots and Woolrich hiking shorts that were becoming accepted casual wear, especially among the restless young. As urbanites sought escape and tried their legs in deserts and mountains, they saw exactly what Abbey was talking about. The tinsel of industrialized America was spreading over their last refuges. Despite their efforts, the dismantling of nature was going on at a far faster pace than its preservation. His concerns — based on the quieter warnings of a long line of noted conservationists — culminated in an anger that sparked and magnified their own. "Mr. Abbey is a good hater," chortled the urbane but conservation-minded *New Yorker.*

But Ed Abbey was not their leader. He left that to the administrative geniuses, the David Browers of the movement. The largely voiceless rank and file sat through wilderness hearings and supported legislation in the face of frequent defeats at the hands of the politically powerful exploiters. Meanwhile, this flamboyant Pancho Villa storming out of the badlands for verbal blasts at the megamachine became their hero, a hero whose panache, because at times zany and laughable, though in essence serious, gave them heart in what they saw as a grim life-and-death struggle over the earth's future. He has given buoyancy and popular raciness to a volunteer movement always in danger of slipping into gloom, and he has inspired other public figures, such as fellow Utahan Robert Redford, to mount their own campaigns to save wilderness, though using somewhat more restrained methods than Abbey seems to suggest. And if conservation organizations remain solidly nonviolent, they are grateful to Abbey, whose diatribes draw the fire that opponents of conservation once heaped on their heads, who makes them and their goals seem staid and reasonable by comparison.

After the success of *Desert Solitaire,* Abbey's writing fortunes improved. *Harper's, Playboy, Life* — even *The Reader's Digest* — wanted his articles for a public eager to follow environmental affairs, eager for vicarious thrills via the wilderness curmudgeon. He was in demand to write the oversized, full-color nature books gracing the coffee tables of middle America. In 1973 Time-Life Books published *Cactus Country* and E. P. Dutton his *Appalachian Wilderness,* each graced with lavish photographs. Two years earlier the Sierra Club had sponsored *Slickrock: The Canyon Country of Southeast Utah.* The volume was designed to win public sympathy for preserving Abbey's desert stamping grounds. The feisty, aggressive style of *Slickrock* helped defeat several industrial invasions, such as the Kaiparowits power plant, though the energy industry continues to eye environmentally careless Utah as a prime site for the polluting generating plants unwanted by more progressive states.

Within the sales and propaganda success of *Slickrock* lay an irony that the *New York Times* was quick to point out. David Brower had been forced to resign as the Club's leader because of his militancy. Now the organization was sponsoring "a two-fisted polemic against 'industrial tourism.' " The book, more warlike than any Brower had edited, was a sign of how far the movement, helped by Abbey, had shifted in just two years.

Abbey's most recent book, *The Journey Home* (1977), collects a series of essays ranging geographically from a lookout tower in Montana to the Hoboken waterfront. In places it boils with the expected Abbey ire, but the author also is at ease playing his flute to the evening or talking quietly to a grove of aspens — literary risks that could easily slide into bathos if attempted by a less skilled hand. Along with the Indians who once inhabited the region around Wolf Hole, Edward Abbey considers this area the navel of creation. Brooding on the changing world from his last stand, he shows the flexibility and talent to expand and deepen his vision, continuing to delight and surprise his readers. Garth McCann sums up the Westerner's contributions to literature and conservation: "On the whole, Abbey's writings have brought the West spiritually into the present — away from the pseudo-cowboyism and ill-considered individualism that pervade popular notions, and into the problems, the personalities, and the forces that constitute the limits, the threats, and the options for our time. The issue is no longer whether the good guys will beat bad guys, whether the settlers will prevail against the ranchers, or whether the sheriff will catch the crook. Today we must ask whether the people generally and individually can adjust their culture to their needs and to those of their environment.... Will we damn our entire existence in order to create a temporary pleasure-dome, or will we be able to make the most of the contradictory values and conditions within which we must survive?"

Jackson Hole Country of Grand Teton National Park. "I am always glad to touch the living rock again and dip my head in high mountain air." – *John Muir.* Wyoming Travel Commission.

Chapter 17

Discovering Ourselves

In a dark time, the eye begins to see....

— Theodore Roethke

On July 16, 1945, a new dawn rose over the world. Its white fireball blotted out the delicate morning colors that each day for thousands of years had streaked the mountains and slowly stretched over the deserts around Alamogordo, New Mexico. Hunched in their bunkers, some scientists feared that the heat from the first atomic blast would ignite the hydrogen and nitrogen that wrap the earth, igniting a wildfire that would leap around the lands and seas of the globe. That first and last worldwide conflagration did not occur, but since then men have lived in fear of the miraculous invention of their own hands.

It was a dramatic event that has become seared on civilization's consciousness. Many writers mark the beginning of the Age of Ecology with that date and with that

199

onset of fear. Yet the fireball that throws its shadows over our future in a world now constantly in danger of nuclear war is symbolic rather than definitive. For thousands of years in less dramatic ways cultures have had the ability to destroy their earth and themselves along with it. Parts of northern Africa, once the breadbasket of Roman legions, now are unproductive desert. Spain's arid plateau owes its bleak condition more to overgrazing by sheep than to the vicissitudes of the weather. The delicate topsoil of many of our own Western ranges is blowing away, not because of a lack of rain but because of our preference for quick profits. In recent times, technology has increased the possibilities of our doing ourselves in. The pesticides, air pollution, water waste, and overpopulation upsetting the planet's vital balance might lead a dispassionate observer to conclude that man is making war on himself.

The fact that the first atomic detonation occurred in the West might be largely coincidental, but not entirely so: the West was where the space was to test the new invention. In a way, then, the explosion is a culmination of our European culture, of the nervous Westward movement, the successes and failures of a technological culture based on constant expansion trying its ways out on a habitat that was thought to be infinitely forgiving, that was so vast it could be mined, lumbered, populated, and grazed without thought for the future.

In the last hundred years or so — a mere twinkling of the eye as time goes — we have radically altered the ecosystems of half a continent from the relatively stable conditions prevailing for thousands of years. If the West's land and resources were unlimited, there would be no conservation movement, but we now know that the earth no longer is as large or as forgiving as our grandfathers supposed. As Louis Simpson remarks in the epigraph of this book, we have come to the end of the open road, and the assumptions our civilization used to get there no

longer apply — in the West, or, for that matter, on the rest
of our small planet. Arriving in California, the pioneers
saw only the empty Pacific before them. We have turned
our wagons around from the brink of the continent and
have come to ourselves, to the realization that our physical and spiritual welfare are bound up with the nature we
have readily abused. This coming to ourselves, this evalu-
ation of where we have come from and where we are going,
can be a painful process. Yet whether in our personal lives
or in the broader environmental affairs that concern all of
us, coming to ourselves is a necessity if we are to see our
way with hope into the future.

At once the disturbing and humbling perspective raises
more questions than we can immediately answer. The
unlimited possibilities and opportunities that the technology of our time seems to promise come accompanied by
equally unlimited uncertainties and fears. Given the
sweep of geology, measured in millions of years, man has
been on the earth only a short while, and it is not written
anywhere that he is destined to remain. When accepting
the Nobel Prize, William Faulkner may well have been
wrong in stating that man not only will endure but prevail. It may well be that the very drive to prevail, to
dominate, will mean his end, as the Greeks feared over
two thousand years ago. Perhaps, with other species, his
time to flourish is limited, as was that of the dinosaur and
the mammoth. Even today the California condor dwindles
toward extinction in the Los Padres National Forest near
Los Angeles, our largest Western city. It may be — despite
the rantings of Gifford Pinchot or the gentle rebukes of
Joseph Wood Krutch — that our fate lies not with ourselves but in the stars, or at any rate with forces we can
barely perceive, that lie beyond our control.

Yet, if as Edward Abbey says in his introduction, our
ability to "reason, experiment, and communicate" is what
distinguishes man from other creatures, we also have

some thrilling alternatives, made more thrilling by the very possibility that we might fail.

Ecology has been called the Subversive Science because it raises such doubts, because it calls into question not only our personal day-to-day dealings and attitudes toward our surroundings but the larger functions of culture — the political, commercial, and industrial matrix of which we are all, like it or not, inextricably a part. To attempt an escape to the woods, as was the fashion some years ago, living close to the land and independent of society, is a romantic delusion, a dream no longer possible. The American hinterland is gone. Yet to change the modus operandi of a powerful society that at least since the Renaissance has been moving toward the conglomerate as its ultimate expression seems too large an order; to gnash our teeth at the realization is fruitless. What, then, can we do?

In the very phrasing of the question lies part of the answer. A restless, nervous people, we are addicted to earth movers, chain saws, and computers, the objects that we feel save us from chaos. We are compelled to meet each perceived problem with an aggressive, technological solution. When a river sweeps houses from its natural floodplain, we call for dams and federal money to rebuild on the same site. When we begin to run short of oil or timber, we demand that our technocrats drill more wells and invade virgin forests, instead of questioning the waste that has made us the gluttons of the world. As Olaus Murie knew too well during his years in the Biological Survey, the hardest thing for Americans to do is to let nature alone, to see themselves as part of nature's context and to live as simply as practicable in it. The stubborn attitude is changing. Slowly we are expanding Wilderness Areas, replacing biocides with mantises and ladybugs, the natural enemies of some garden pests. Fortunately, Steward Udall's pronouncement, which rattled home folk back in rural St. Johns, that "posterity will honor us more for the roads and dams we do not build . . . than for those we do," no longer seems as shocking as it did in 1968, a mere ten years ago. Letting nature alone, even restoring it to its former wildness, is becoming an accepted option, a notion that would have bewildered the struggling pioneers.

The crux of the dilemma is whether or not we can learn to control our addiction to technology. Despite other objections, Joseph Wood Krutch praised technology when used to relieve human suffering. We cringe imagining the frontiersman with an abscessed tooth or a ruptured appendix. The technological advances in medicine — x-rays, antibiotics, anesthetics — make us pity those just a few generations ago who suffered through what for us are inconveniences rather than disasters. Given the many benefits, the problem is that we have not yet learned to use technology just enough, or when not to use it at all. That is a problem of good and evil; religious leaders and philosophers have been dealing with it for millenia with, at best, only a modicum of success. It may be we will never learn.

It may be that we will be forced to learn, not through enlightenment but necessity. Recent droughts throughout the West have forced us to come to terms with profligacy in one respect at least. To their amazement, people in Los Angeles and San Francisco have found that they can survive as happy, loving, working, civilized creatures without brimming swimming pools and daily baths. And the recent high prices of oil and nuclear energy are forcing those who have cared not one whit about clean air to consider the advantages of solar power. We are, we like to tell ourselves, a practical people. And we may be learning, as Professor E. F. Schumacher phrased it, that small can be beautiful as well as economically expedient, that unplanned urban growth and sprawl into the suburbs spell financial madness and social disruption that we all must pay for with higher taxes. And by similar tokens we might grow to realize that we are a healthier, happier, if not richer, people without junk foods, freeways, and a televison in every bedroom — that there is a certain beauty in leanness, in coming to ourselves and our individual resources. Up to now we have blundered along, making do with a crisis mentality. We have preferred, as the popular metaphor goes, Band-Aids and aspirin to major surgery. The question is whether society can make the shift to more sensible ways before the planet's health reaches the point of no return.

In one sense, there is a curious and schizoid contradiction in this question of progress. If there is anything radical in our culture, it is not the preservation of nature, as has been alleged. Rather it lies in the degree that our technological society has negated the early Dream of the Garden — at least that part of the dream concerning a satisfying life in the midst of natural abundance. President Jefferson envisioned a nation based on independent and enlightened yeomen farmers. In a twisted way, the dream lives on in the continuing view of nature as an unlimited, exploitable treasure house. During hunting season the woods are frighteningly full of urbanites desperately acting out their part of the fantasy. That our country has not developed according to the ideal of the Peaceable Kingdom hardly seems arguable. In fact, as our history developed, the fulfillment of the dream became impossible. Overpopulation alone has made it so — witness again the droves of frantic hunters. Still, the vision has its positive side, the view of a country prospering within its natural advantages and limits, not only prospering materially but spiritually through its relationship with a natural world treasured and respected rather than abused.

This idea Western conservationists — goaded by their vision and often scorned as unpatriotic — preached a hundred years ago and have continued to preach long after the nation reduced its garden to a few remnant plots. In this sense at least, conservationists have been the real conservatives, urging restoration to past ideals of balance. Academics perhaps have not given sufficient recognition either to the social impact or the literary merit of conservationists' writing. Their books combine science, sensitivity, and deep personal commitment, giving a new turn to the genre of nature writing inherited from Europe. Conservationists' most effective expression, however, came from the citizen groups they founded: John Muir's Sierra Club, Aldo Leopold's Wilderness Society, and David Brower's Friends of the Earth. The accomplishments of these groups, in changing laws, establishing wildlife and forest reserves, and generally moving a reluctant nation, verge on the miraculous when viewed in light of the obstacles. Theirs have been labors of vision and love, succeeding because ordinary citizens volunteered their time and money, with the gains going to future generations — a rare phenomenon in human history and a triumph for grass-roots democracy. They have pitted themselves not only against industry and government but against the whole boom and bust psychology of a young and careless nation. At every turn they have been at a disadvantage, paying their own way to testify at hearings, sleeping on the living-room floors of friends, digging into their own pockets to scrape together $20,000 for an ad in the *New York Times* or the *Washington Post*. This in contrast to the comfortable army of lobbyists and the lavish, tax-deductible publicity campaigns funded by the exponents of personal gain at any cost to the nation. Without these citizen groups we would have no national parks, no clean-air standards, no more whooping cranes, grizzlies, or golden eagles — the sum of our remaining wild heritage that much of the public takes for granted. The debt to them can never be paid, only honored by the concern of others.

That concern is needed on the national as well as the local level. As the population, and along with it the industrial web of the country, grows, areas once protected by isolation are threatened. In some cases the national parks are desperately short of funds to add areas which would protect the integrity of ecosystems. The Forest Service, with its emphasis on economic use rather than preservation, always bears watching. The millions of acres administered by the Bureau of Land Management hardly have been watched at all — though the Bureau's domain includes some of the nation's most stunning scenery and essential habitat for such threatened species as the bighorn sheep. All three agencies now are involved in selecting wild land to be preserved under the provisions of the Wilderness Act. Their past performances have tended to favor those wishing to exploit the public's land rather than enjoy it. The preserved legacies they currently administer exist only because citizens, especially local citizens, went out of their way, testifying at hearings and writing their Congressmen, to blunt the influence of special interests. A list of other areas needing citizen concern can go on almost indefinitely: air-pollution standards, land-use planning for communities, nuclear safety, pesticide regulation, solar development, threatened wildlife.... Yet beyond these specific issues is the larger question Mr. Abbey appropriately raises in his introduction: whether the descendants of the conservationists discussed in the preceding chapters can survive in a system that increasingly decides the shape of the future on the basis of economic power.

The messages of conservationists are as diverse as their voices — from the practical economics of Gifford Pinchot to the mysticism of Mary Hunter Austin. One general truth we can learn from their collective urgings: diversity, rather than narrowness, marks a healthy state in nature as well as in human affairs. That message touches on our whole humanistic and democratic tradition, not just on conservation, but it goes against the regimentation encouraged by the computer age. Still, even a sulfurous critic of society like Edward Abbey sees hope for true progress if we have the strength to insist on a different course by avoiding "the Expand and Expire theory of human endeavor." In this respect, we are fortunate here in the West because much of our original natural heritage remains intact, a basis for future progress. The public has come to see Colorado's Long's Peak and the national park that surrounds and protects it as one of the greatest assets this increasingly populated and industrialized state can have. It has seen Big Bend National Park in Texas restore itself from a gouged and overgrazed dust bowl to a wonder of natural desert vegetation and wildlife. It is discovering, with a new, enlightened pride in Western regionalism, that mistakes can be corrected. These parks should not be simply curiosities and relics of nature but models for implementing a new ethic of care throughout the West.

Basically, then, the question is whether our society will follow through in even more difficult and complex times with what the people in this book started only a short time ago. Will it be flexible and humble and caring enough to adjust to the new realities we have suddenly found confronting us at the end of the open road? Will we be wise enough to leave ourselves substantial margins of error in deciding whether to protect or destroy the California condor, to build or not to build another dam in the Grand Canyon, to stripmine or not to waste forever the productivity of a wheat farm? Or will our culture, as others have done in the past, demand that every last penny of profit be squeezed from the earth as quickly as possible, regardless of consequences ten, twenty, or a hundred years from now?

As David Brower pointed out, that process will be one of
the most exciting discoveries we have made about ourselves, and the decisions along the way will be the most
critical man has ever made about his future on the earth.

*Debris after a modern logging operation. Once the land lay
pristine from ocean to ocean.* High Country News.

Selected Bibliography

CHAPTER 1
Visions and Revisions:
Conservation Begins in the American West

Bates, J. Leonard. "Fulfilling American Democracy: The Conservation Movement, 1907-1921." *Mississippi Valley Historical Review,* 44 (1957), 29-57.

Billington, Ray Allen. *The Far Western Frontier: 1830-1860.* New York: Harper, 1956.

Boyton, Percy H. *The Rediscovery of the Frontier.* Chicago: University of Chicago Press, 1931.

Brooks, Paul. *The View from Lincoln Hill: Man and the Land in a New England Town.* Boston: Houghton Mifflin, 1976.

Carson, Rachel. *Silent Spring.* Boston: Houghton Mifflin, 1962.

Clark, William, and Meriwether Lewis. *The Journals of Lewis and Clark.* Ed. Bernard DeVoto. Boston: Houghton Mifflin, 1953.

Clawson, Marion. *Uncle Sam's Acres.* New York: Dodd, Mead, 1951.

Clissold, Stephen. *The Seven Cities of Cíbola.* London:Eyre and Spottiswoode, 1961.

Coyle, David C. *Conservation: An American Story of Conflict and Accomplishment.* New Brunswick, New Jersey: Rutgers University Press, 1957.

De Voss, David. "What Ever Happened to California?" *Time,* 110 (July 18, 1977), 22-23.

DeVoto, Bernard. *Across the Wide Missouri.* Boston: Houghton Mifflin, 1947.

―――. *The Course of Empire.* Boston: Houghton Mifflin, 1952.

―――. *The Year of Decision: 1846.* Boston: Little, Brown, 1943.

Dobie, J. Frank. *The Voice of the Coyote.* Boston: Little, Brown, 1949.

Douglas, William O. *The Three Hundred Year War: A Chronicle of Ecological Disaster.* New York: Random House, 1972.

Ehrlich, Paul R.; Anne H. Ehrlich; and John P. Holdren. *Ecoscience: Population, Resources, Environment.* San Francisco: W. H. Freeman, 1977.

Ellis, David M., Ed. *The Frontier in American Development.* Ithaca: Cornell University Press, 1969.

Fleming, Donald. "Roots of the New Conservation Movement." *Perspectives in American History,* Vol. 6, Cambridge, Massachusetts: Harvard University Press, 1972.

Foerster, Norman. *Nature in American Literature.* New York: Macmillan, 1923.

Frome, Michael. *Battle for the Wilderness.* New York: Praeger, 1974.

Goetzman, William H. *Army Exploration in the American West: 1803-1863.* New Haven: Yale University Press, 1959.

Graham, Frank, Jr. *Man's Dominion: The Story of Conservation in America.* New York: M. Evans, 1971.

"The Great and Wild Californicated West." *Time,* 100 (August 21, 1972), 15.

King, Clarence. *Mountaineering in the Sierra Nevada.* Ed. Francis P. Farquhar. New York: W. W. Norton, 1935.

Kollmorgen, Walter M. "The Woodsman's Assaults on the Domain of the Cattlemen." *Annals of the Association of American Geographers,* 59 (1969), 215-39.

Lanham, Url. *The Bone Hunters.* New York: Columbia University Press, 1973.

McCarthy, G. Michael. *Hour of Trial: The Conservation Conflict in Colorado and the West, 1891-1907.* Norman: University of Oklahoma Press, 1977.

—————. "The Pharisee Spirit: Gifford Pinchot in Colorado." *Pennsylvania Magazine of History and Biography,* 97 (July 1973), 362-78.

Malin, James C. *The Grassland of North America: Prolegomena to its History.* rev. ed. Lawrence, Kansas, 1956.

Marsh, George Perkins. *Man and Nature.* rpt. Cambridge, Massachusetts: Harvard University Press, 1965.

Nash, Roderick. "The American Cult of the Primitive." *American Quarterly,* 18 (1966), 517-37.

—————. *The American Environment: Readings in the History of Conservation.* Reading, Massachusetts: Addison-Wesley, 1968.

—————. *Wilderness and the American Mind.* rev. ed. New Haven: Yale University Press, 1973.·

Peffer, E. Louise. *The Closing of the Public Domain: Disposal and Reservation Policies, 1900-50.* Stanford: Stanford University Press, 1951.

Reingold, Nathan. *Science in Nineteenth-century America: A Documentary History.* New York: Hill and Wang, 1964.

Richardson, Elmo R. *The Politics of Conservation: Crusades and Controversies, 1897-1913.* Berkeley: University of California Press, 1962.

Robbins, Roy M. *Our Landed Heritage: The Public Domain, 1776-1970.* 2nd. rev. ed. Lincoln University of Nebraska Press, 1976.

Schmitt, Peter J. *Back to Nature: The Arcadian Myth in Urban America*. New York: Oxford University Press, 1969.

Schwartz, William, Ed. *Voices for the Wilderness*. New York: Ballantine Books, 1969.

Sibley, George. "The Desert Empire." *Harper's*, 255 (October 1977), 49-56, 61-68.

Sierra Club Bulletin, 61 (October 1976). A special issue on the history and preservation of America's wilderness.

Smith, Frank E. *The Politics of Conservation*. New York: Pantheon, 1966.

Smith, Henry Nash. *Virgin Land: The American West as Symbol and Myth*. Cambridge, Massachusetts: Harvard University Press, 1975.

Stegner, Wallace. *Angle of Repose*. Garden City, New York: Doubleday, 1971.

————. *Beyond the Hundredth Meridian: John Wesley Powell and the Second Opening of the West*. Boston: Houghton Mifflin, 1954.

Strong, Douglas H. *The Conservationists*. Reading, Massachusetts: Addison-Wesley, 1971.

Taft, Robert. *Artists and Illustrators of the Old West: 1850-1900*. New York: Charles Scribner's Sons, 1953.

Trefethen, James B. *Crusade for Wildlife: Highlights in Conservation Progress*. Harrisburg, Pennsylvania: The Stackpole Company, 1961.

Turner, Frederick Jackson. *The Frontier in American History*. New York: Henry Holt, 1920.

Udall, Stewart. *The Quiet Crisis*. New York: Holt, Rinehart and Winston, 1963.

Wallace, Edward S. *The Great Reconnaissance: Soldiers, Artists, and Scientists on the Frontier, 1848-1861*. Boston: Little, Brown, 1955.

Watkins, T. H., and Charles S. Watson, Jr. *The Land No One Knows: America and the Public Domain*. San Francisco: Sierra Club, 1975.

Webb, Walter Prescott. *The Great Frontier*. rev. ed. Austin: University of Texas Press, 1964.

————. *The Great Plains*. Boston: Ginn and Company, 1931.

Wilkins, Thurman. *Clarence King: A Biography*. New York: Macmillan, 1958.

Worster, Donald, Ed. *American Environmentalism: The Formative Period, 1860-1915*. New York: Wiley, 1973.

————. *Nature's Economy: The Roots of Ecology*. San Francisco: Sierra Club, 1977.

CHAPTER 2
John Wesley Powell and the Rediscovery
of the West: Running Rivers and Bureaucracies

The Colorado River Region and John Wesley Powell: A Collection of Papers Honoring Powell on the 100th Anniversary of his Exploration of the Colorado River, 1869-1969. Washington: U.S. Government Printing Office, 1969.

Darrah, William Culp. *Powell of the Colorado*. Princeton: Princeton University Press, 1951.

Powell, John Wesley. *Canyons of the Colorado*. Meadville, Pennsylvania: Flood and Vincent, 1895.

————. *Exploration of the Colorado River of the West and its Tributaries*. Washington: U.S. Government Printing Office, 1875.

————. *Report on the Lands of the Arid Region of the United States*. Washington: U.S. Government Printing Office, 1878.

————. *Selected Prose of John Wesley Powell*. Ed. George Crossette. Boston: David R. Godine, 1970.

————, Ed. *Contributions to North American Ethnology*, Vol. 1-7, 9. Washington: U.S. Government Printing Office, 1877-1893.

Reingold, Nathan. *Science in Nineteenth-century America: A Documentary History.* New York: Hill and Wang, 1964.

Stegner, Wallace. *Beyond the Hundredth Meridian: John Wesley Powell and the Second Opening of the West.* Boston: Houghton Mifflin, 1954.

Terrell, John Upton. *The Man Who Rediscovered America: A Biography of John Wesley Powell.* New York: Weybright and Talley, 1969.

Wilkins, Thurman. *Clarence King: A Biography.* New York: Macmillan, 1958.

CHAPTER 3
The Mysteries of the Mountains and Practical Politics: John Muir Fights for His Range of Light

Arden, Harvey. "John Muir's Wild America." *National Geographic,* 143 (April 1973), 433-61.

Earl, John. *John Muir's Longest Walk.* Garden City, New York: Doubleday, 1975.

Johnson, Robert Underwood. *Remembered Yesterdays.* Boston: Little, Brown, 1923.

Jones, Holway R. *John Muir and the Sierra Club: The Battle for Yosemite.* San Francisco: Sierra Club, 1965.

Lyon, Thomas J. *John Muir.* Boise, Idaho: Boise State College Western Writers Series, 1972.

Muir, John. "The American Forests." *The Atlantic Monthly,* 80 (August 1897), 145-57.

————. *John of the Mountains: The Unpublished Journals of John Muir.* Ed. Linnie Marsh Wolfe. Boston: Houghton Mifflin, 1938.

————. *The Mountains of California.* New York: The Century Company, 1911.

————. *My First Summer in the Sierra.* Boston: Houghton Mifflin, 1911.

———. *Our National Parks*. Boston: Houghton Mifflin, 1901.

———. *Stickeen*. Boston: Houghton Mifflin, 1909.

———. *The Story of My Boyhood and Youth*. Boston: Houghton Mifflin, 1913.

———. *A Thousand-Mile Walk to the Gulf*. Boston: Houghton Mifflin, 1916.

———. *Travels in Alaska*. Boston: Houghton Mifflin, 1915.

———. *The Wilderness World of John Muir*. Ed. Edwin Way Teale. Boston: Houghton Mifflin, 1976.

———. *Works: The Sierra Edition*. Ed. William F. Bade. 10 Vols. Boston: Houghton Mifflin, 1917-1924.

———. *The Yosemite*. New York: The Century Company, 1912.

Smith, Herbert F. *John Muir*. New York: Twayne Publishers, 1965.

Watkins, T. H. *John Muir's America*. New York: Crown, 1976.

Wolfe, Linnie Marsh. *Son of the Wilderness: The Life of John Muir*. New York: Knopf, 1945.

Young, Samuel Hall. *Alaska Days with John Muir*. New York: Fleming H. Revell Company, 1915.

CHAPTER 4
Gifford Pinchot, Aristocrat: Progressive Politics and Despotism Create the National Forests

Barney, Daniel R. *The Last Stand: Ralph Nader's Study Group Report on the National Forests*. New York: Grossman, 1974.

Bates, J. Leonard. "Fulfilling American Democracy: The Conservation Movement, 1907-1921." *Mississippi Valley Historical Review,* 44 (1957), 29-57.

Cutright, Paul R. *Theodore Roosevelt the Naturalist*. New York: Harper and Brothers, 1956.

216

Fausold, Martin L. *Gifford Pinchot: Bull Moose Progressive.* Syracuse: Syracuse University Press, 1961.

Frome, Michael. *The Forest Service.* New York: Praeger, 1971.

————. *Whose Woods These Are: The Story of the National Forests.* Garden City, New York: Doubleday, 1962.

Hays, Samuel P. *Conservation and the Gospel of Efficiency: The Progressive Conservation Movement, 1890-1920.* Cambridge, Massachusetts: Harvard University Press, 1959.

Janson, Lone E. *The Copper Spike.* Anchorage, Alaska: Alaska Northwest Publishing Company, 1975.

McCarthy, G. Michael. *Hour of Trial: The Conservation Conflict in Colorado and the West, 1891-1907.* Norman: University of Oklahoma Press, 1977.

————. "The Pharisee Spirit: Gifford Pinchot in Colorado." *Pennsylvania Magazine of History and Biography,* 97 (July 1973), 362-78.

McGeary, Martin Nelson. *Gifford Pinchot: Forester-Politician.* Princeton: Princeton University Press, 1960.

Marsh, George Perkins. *Man and Nature.* rpt. Cambridge, Massachusetts: Harvard University Press, 1965.

Penick, James L. *Progressive Politics and Conservation: The Ballinger-Pinchot Affair.* Chicago: University of Chicago Press, 1968.

Pinchot, Gifford. *Biltmore Forest.* rpt. New York: Arno, 1970.

————. *Breaking New Ground.* New York: Harcourt, Brace, 1947.

————. *The Fight for Conservation.* New York: Doubleday, Page, 1910.

Pinkett, Harold T. *Gifford Pinchot: Private and Public Forester.* Urbana: University of Illinois Press, 1970.

Richardson, Elmo R. *The Politics of Conservation: Crusades and Controversies, 1897-1913.* Berkeley: University of California Press, 1962.

Roosevelt, Theodore. *Theodore Roosevelt: An Autobiography.* New York: Macmillan, 1913.

Shepherd, Jack. *The Forest Killers: The Destruction of the American Wilderness.* New York: Weybright and Talley, 1975.

Wood, Harold W., Jr. "Pinchot and Mather: How the Forest Service and Park Service Got that Way." *Not Man Apart* (Mid-December 1976), 1, 13.

CHAPTER 5
Stephen Mather: A Borax Millionaire
Rescues the National Parks

Albright, Horace, and Frank Taylor. *Oh, Ranger!* Stanford: Stanford University Press, 1928.

Buck, Paul H. *The Evolution of the National Park System of the United States.* Washington: U.S. Government Printing Office, 1946.

Chittenden, Hiram. *The Yellowstone National Park.* rpt. Norman: University of Oklahoma Press, 1971.

Cramton, Louis C. *Early History of Yellowstone National Park and Its Relation to National Park Policies.* Washington: U.S. Government Printing Office, 1932.

Darling, Frank Fraser, and Noel D. Eichhorn. *Man and Nature in the National Parks.* Washington, D.C.: Conservation Foundation, 1969.

DeVoto, Bernard. "Let's Close the National Parks." *Harper's,* 207 (October 1953), 49-52.

Everhart, William C. *The National Park Service.* New York: Praeger, 1972.

Hampton, H. Duane. *How the U.S. Cavalry Saved Our National Parks.* Bloomington: Indiana University Press, 1971.

Ise, John. *Our National Park Policy: A Critical History.* Baltimore: Johns Hopkins University Press, 1961.

Mather, Stephen. *Progress in the Development of the National Parks.* Washington: U.S. Government Printing Office, 1916.

Roper, Laura Wood. *F. L. O.: A Biography of Frederick Law Olmsted.* Baltimore: Johns Hopkins University Press, 1974.

Russell, Carl P. *One Hundred Years in Yosemite: The Story of a Great Park and Its Friends.* rev. ed. Berkeley: University of California Press, 1947.

Sax, Joseph L. "America's National Parks: Their Principles, Purposes, and Prospects." *Natural History,* 85 (October 1976), 57-88.

Shankland, Robert. *Steve Mather of the National Parks.* New York: Knopf, 1951.

Sutton, Ann, and Myron Sutton. *Guarding the Treasured Lands: The Story of the National Park Service.* Philadelphia: J. B. Lippincott, 1965.

Wood, Harold W., Jr. "Pinchot and Mather: How the Forest Service and Park Service Got that Way." *Not Man Apart* (Mid-December 1976), 1, 13.

CHAPTER 6
Enos Mills: Propagandist of the Rocky Mountains

Dannen, Kent. "Rocky Mountain Man." *Westways,* 68 (August 1976), 27-30.

Hawthorne, Hildegarde, and Esther Burnell Mills. *Enos Mills of the Rockies.* New York: Houghton Mifflin, 1935.

Mills, Enos. *The Adventures of a Nature Guide.* Garden City, New York: Doubleday, Page, 1920.

———. *The Grizzly: Our Greatest Wild Animal.* Boston: Houghton Mifflin, 1919.

————. *In Beaver World*. Boston: Houghton Mifflin, 1913.

————. *The Spell of the Rockies*. Boston: Houghton Mifflin, 1911.

————. *The Story of Estes Park and a Guide Book*. Denver: Outdoor Life Publishing Company, 1905.

————. *Waiting in the Wilderness*. Garden City, New York: Doubleday, Page, 1922.

————. *Wild Life on the Rockies*. Boston: Houghton Mifflin, 1909.

————. *Your National Parks*. Boston: Houghton Mifflin, 1917.

"Monopolies in National Parks." Des Moines *Sunday Capital,* December 19, 1920, p. 8-A.

Phillips, Grace D. "Guardian of the Rockies." *National Parks Magazine,* 29 (January-March 1955), 9-15.

Shankland, Robert. *Steve Mather of the National Parks*. New York: Knopf, 1951.

CHAPTER 7
Mary Hunter Austin Sees God Under A Walnut Tree

Austin, Mary. *The American Rhythm*. Boston: Houghton Mifflin, 1930.

————. *The Arrow Maker: A Drama in Three Acts*. New York: Duffield and Company, 1911.

————. "Beyond the Hudson," *Saturday Review,* 7 (December 6, 1930), 432, 444.

————. *Earth Horizon*. Boston: Houghton Mifflin, 1932.

————. *The Flock*. Boston: Houghton Mifflin, 1906.

————. *The Ford*. Boston: Houghton Mifflin, 1917.

220

―――. *Isidro. Boston:* Houghton Mifflin, 1905.

―――. *The Land of Journeys' Ending.* New York: The Century Company, 1924.

―――. *The Land of Little Rain.* Boston: Houghton Mifflin, 1950.

―――. *Lost Borders.* New York: Harper and Brothers, 1909.

―――. *One-Smoke Stories.* Boston: Houghton Mifflin, 1934.

Barker, Ruth Laughlin. "Interesting Westerners." *Sunset,* 43 (September 1919), 49-50.

Doyle, Helen MacKnight. *Mary Austin: Woman of Genius.* New York: Gotham House, 1939.

DuBois, Arthur E. "Mary Hunter Austin: 1868-1934." *Southwest Review,* 20 (April 1935), 231-264.

Houghland, Willard, Ed. *Mary Austin: A Memorial.* Santa Fe, New Mexico: Laboratory of Anthropology, 1944.

Lyday, Jo W. *Mary Austin: The Southwest Works.* Austin: Steck-Vaughn Company, 1968.

Pearce, Thomas Matthews. *The Beloved House.* Caldwell, Idaho: The Caxton Printers, 1940.

―――. *Mary Hunter Austin.* New York: Twayne Publishers, 1965.

Sergeant, Elizabeth Shepley. "Mary Austin: A Portrait." *Saturday Review,* 11 (September 8, 1934), 96.

Smith, Henry. "The Feel of the Purposeful Earth: Mary Austin's Prophecy." *New Mexico Quarterly,* 1 (February, 1931), 17-33.

Starr, Kevin. "Mary Austin: Mystic, Writer, Conservationist." *Sierra Club Bulletin,* 61 (November-December 1976), 34-6.

Stegner, Wallace. *Angle of Repose.* Garden City, New York: Doubleday, 1971.

White, Gilbert. *The Natural History of Selborne.* New York: D. Appleton and Company, 1895.

CHAPTER 8
The Move Toward Holism: "Thinking Like A Mountain,"
Aldo Leopold Breaks with the Forest Service

Brower, David, Ed. *The Sierra Club Wilderness Handbook*. New York:Ballantine Books, 1967.

Douglas, William O. *A Wilderness Bill of Rights*. Boston: Little, Brown, 1965.

Errington, Paul L. "In Appreciation of Aldo Leopold." *Journal of Wildlife Management,* 12 (October 1948), 341-50.

Flader, Susan. *The Sand Country of Aldo Leopold*. San Francisco: Sierra Club, 1973.

————. *Thinking Like a Mountain: Aldo Leopold and the Evolution of an Ecological Attitude toward Deer, Wolves, and Forests*. Columbia: University of Missouri Press, 1974.

Frome, Michael. *Battle for the Wilderness*. New York: Praeger, 1974.

Iltis, Hugh. "We Need Many More Scientific Areas." *Wisconsin Conservation Bulletin,* 24 (September 1959), 3-8.

Leopold, Aldo. *Game Management*. New York: Charles Scribner's Sons, 1933.

————. "Origins and Ideals of Wilderness." *The Living Wilderness,* 5 (July 1940), 7.

————. *Round River: From the Journals of Aldo Leopold*. Ed. Luna Leopold. New York: Oxford University Press, 1953.

————. *A Sand County Almanac and Sketches Here and There*. New York: Oxford University Press, 1949.

Nash, Roderick. *Wilderness and the American Mind*. rev. ed. New Haven: Yale University Press, 1973.

Schriver, Edward. "Leopold's Land Ethic: Wishful Thinking or Workable Dream?" *Sierra Club Bulletin,* 62 (March 1977), 9-11, 16.

Schwartz, William, Ed. *Voices for the Wilderness*. New York: Ballantine Books, 1969.

Sierra Club Bulletin, 61 (October 1976). A special issue on the history and preservation of America's wilderness.

Stone, Christopher D. *Should Trees Have Standing?: Toward Legal Rights for Natural Objects.* Los Altos, California: William Kaufman, Inc., 1974.

Trefethen, James B. *Crusade for Wildlife: Highlights in Conservation Progress.* Harrisburg, Pennsylvania: The Stackpole Company, 1961.

CHAPTER 9
Bernard DeVoto: On the Barricades

Clark, William, and Meriwether Lewis. *The Journals of Lewis and Clark.* Ed. Bernard DeVoto. Boston: Houghton Mifflin, 1953.

DeVoto, Bernard. *Across the Wide Missouri.* Boston: Houghton Mifflin, 1947.

————. *The Course of Empire.* Boston: Houghton Mifflin, 1952.

————. *The Crooked Mile.* New York: Minton, Balch and Company, 1924.

————. *The Easy Chair.* Boston: Houghton Mifflin, 1955.

————. *The Letters of Bernard DeVoto.* Ed. Wallace Stegner. Garden City, New York: Doubleday, 1975.

————. *Mark Twain at Work.* Cambridge, Massachusetts: Harvard University Press, 1942.

————. *Mark Twain's America.* Boston: Little, Brown, 1932.

————. *Mountain Time.* Little, Brown, 1947.

————. *The Year of Decision: 1846.* Boston: Little, Brown, 1943.

Sawey, Orlan. *Bernard DeVoto.* New York: Twayne Publishers, 1969.

Stegner, Wallace. *The Uneasy Chair: A Biography of Bernard DeVoto.* Garden City, New York: Doubleday, 1974.

CHAPTER 10
Science and Sympathy: Olaus Murie and the Fight for Wildlife

Curry, Peggy Simson. "Portrait of a Naturalist." *Audubon,* 65 (November-December 1963), 359-63.

Dobie, J. Frank. *The Voice of the Coyote.* Boston: Little, Brown, 1949.

"1889. . .Olaus J. Murie. . . 1963." *The Living Wilderness,* 84 (Summer-Fall 1963), 3-14.

Heald, Weldon F. "Report from the Gila." *The Living Wilderness.* 17 (Autumn 1952), 26-39.

"The Joys of Solitude and Nature." *Life,* 47 (December 28, 1959), 148-51.

Mitchell, John G. "Where Have All the Tuttu Gone?" *Audubon,* 79 (March 1977), 2-15.

Murie, Adolph. *A Naturalist in Alaska.* Garden City, New York: Doubleday, 1963.

―――. *The Wolves of Mount McKinley.* Washington: U.S. Government Printing Office, 1944.

Murie, Margaret. "Inner Ingredients Inspire Others." *High Country News* (Lander, Wyoming), September 23, 1977, p. 3.

―――. *Island Between.* Fairbanks, Alaska: University of Alaska Press, 1977.

―――. *Two In the Far North.* New York: Knopf, 1962.

―――, and Olaus Murie. *Wapiti Wilderness.* New York: Knopf, 1966.

Murie, Olaus. *Alaska-Yukon Caribou*. Washington: U.S. Government Printing Office, 1935.

————. "Blood Money for School Children." *Audubon*, 58 (May-June 1956), 116-117, 126.

————. "Defending Recreation Areas." *The Living Wilderness*. 14 (Autumn 1949), 22-25.

————. *The Elk of North America*. Harrisburg, Pennsylvania: The Stackpole Company, 1951.

————. *A Field Guide to Animal Tracks*. Boston: Houghton Mifflin, 1954.

————. *Jackson Hole with a Naturalist*. Jackson Hole, Wyoming: Frontier Press, 1963.

————. *Journeys to the Far North*. Palo Alto, California: American West Publishing Company, 1973.

————. "The Last of the Big Bears." *Audubon*, 60 (July-August 1958), 156-158, 188-189.

————. "New Zealand: A First Impression." *Audubon*, 51 (May-June 1949), 172-177.

————. "Our Big Wilderness Cat." *Audubon*, 61 (September-October 1959), 202-203, 229-231, 237.

————. "A Price on His Golden Head." *Audubon*, 54 (July-August 1952), 232-236, 253.

————. "Wolf." *Audubon*, 59 (September-October 1957), 218-221.

————. "Wonder Dog." *Audubon*, 50 (September-October 1948), 268-275.

Trefethen, James B. *Crusade for Wildlife: Highlights in Conservation Progress*. Harrisburg, Pennsylvania: The Stackpole Company, 1961.

Weddle, Ferris M. "Wilderness Champion: Olaus J. Murie," *Audubon*, 52 (July-August 1950), 224-33.

Worster, Donald. *Nature's Economy: The Roots of Ecology*. San Francisco: Sierra Club, 1977.

CHAPTER 11
Joseph Wood Krutch: Quiet Voice for the "Devil's Domain"

Abbey, Edward. "On Nature, the Modern Temper, and the Southwest: An Interview with Joseph Wood Krutch." *Sage,* 2 (Spring 1968), 13-21.

Barzun, Jacques. "An Uncommon Carrier of Truth." *The American Scholar,* 39 (Autumn 1970), 556-57.

Brooks, Atkinson. "The Many Worlds of Joseph Wood Krutch." *Saturday Review,* 53 (July 25, 1970), 17.

Brooks, Paul. *The View from Lincoln Hill: Man and the Land In a New England Town.* Boston: Houghton Mifflin, 1976.

Dubos, René. "The Despairing Optimist." *The American Scholar,* 40 (Winter 1970-1971), 16-20.

Green, Gerald. *An American Prophet.* Garden City, New York: Doubleday, 1977.

Haydn, Hiram. "Joseph Wood Krutch (1893-1970)." *The American Scholar,* 39 (Autumn 1970), 555.

"Joseph Wood Krutch." *New York Times,* May 26, 1970, p. 40.

"Joseph Wood Krutch (1893-1970)." *The Nation,* 210 (June 8, 1970), 677.

"Joseph Wood Krutch, Naturalist, Dies." *New York Times,* May 23, 1970, p. 23.

Krutch, Joseph Wood. *Baja California and the Geography of Hope.* Ed. David Brower. San Francisco: Sierra Club, 1967.

——. *The Best Nature Writing of Joseph Wood Krutch.* New York: Morrow, 1969.

——. *The Best of Two Worlds.* New York: William Sloane Associates, 1953.

——. "Conservation." *Wildlife Review,* 6 (December 1971), 3.

——. *The Desert Year.* New York: William Sloane Associates, 1952.

—————. *The Forgotten Peninsula: A Naturalist in Baja California.* New York: William Sloane Associates, 1961.

—————. *Henry David Thoreau.* New York: William Sloane Associates, 1948.

—————. "If You Don't Mind My Saying So." *The American Scholar,* 39 (Autumn 1970), 558-60.

—————. *The Modern Temper.* New York: Harcourt, Brace, 1929.

—————. *More Lives Than One.* New York: William Sloane Associates, 1962.

—————. "Progress Improves Lands — For What?" Tucson *Arizona Daily Star,* June 19, 1970, p. 8-B.

—————. *The Twelve Seasons.* New York: William Sloane Associates, 1949.

—————. *The Voice of the Desert.* New York: William Sloan Associates, 1955.

Smith, Jeff. "Joseph Wood Krutch, Critic and Scholar, Dies." Tucson *Arizona Daily Star,* May 23, 1970, pp. 1, 4.

CHAPTER 12
Should Trees Have Rights?:
William O. Douglas Expands the Law

Douglas, William O. *Beyond the High Himalayas.* Garden City, New York: Doubleday, 1952.

—————. *Douglas of the Supreme Court: A Selection of His Opinions.* Ed. Vern Countryman. Garden City, New York: Doubleday, 1959.

—————. *Farewell to Texas: A Vanishing Wilderness.* New York: McGraw-Hill, 1967.

—————. *Go East Young Man: The Early Years.* New York: Random House, 1974.

227

—. *My Wilderness: The Pacific West.* Garden City, New York: Doubleday, 1960.

—. *The Three Hundred Year War: A Chronicle of Ecological Disaster.* New York: Random House, 1972.

—. *A Wilderness Bill of Rights.* Boston: Little, Brown, 1965.

Hoffman, John D. "Mr. Justice Douglas' Last Environmental Opinion." *Sierra Club Bulletin,* 61 (May 1976), 8.

"The Last Word." *Time,* 109 (April 11, 1977), 80, 85.

Leopold, Aldo. *A Sand County Almanac and Sketches Here and There.* New York: Oxford University Press, 1949.

Matthews, Tom. "Final Judgment." *Newsweek,* 86 (November 24, 1975), 45-6.

Peer, Elizabeth. "The Mind of a Maverick." *Newsweek,* 86 (November 24, 1975), 46-8.

Stone, Christopher D. *Should Trees Have Standing?: Toward Legal Rights for Natural Objects.* Los Altos, California: William Kaufman, Inc., 1974.

"Tribute." *The New Yorker,* 51 (December 29, 1975), 18-19.

Viorst, Milton. "Bill Douglas Has Never Stopped Fighting the Bullies of Yakima." *New York Times Magazine,* June 14, 1970, pp. 8, 32, 34, 36, 38, 42, 47, 52.

Wayburn, Edgar. "William O. Douglas: A Personal Reminiscence." *Sierra Club Bulletin,* 61 (May 1976), 7-8.

CHAPTER 13
David Brower and Charisma: The Rebirth of the Conservation Movement

Brower, David, Ed. *Gentle Wilderness: The Sierra Nevada.* San Francisco: Sierra Club, 1964.

—. *Grand Canyon: The Threat Is Still Alive.* San Francisco: Sierra Club, 1967.

————. *Not Man Apart: Lines from Robinson Jeffers.* San Francisco: Sierra Club, 1965.

————. *Of All Things Most Yielding.* San Francisco: Friends of the Earth, 1974.

————. *Only a Little Planet.* San Francisco: Friends of the Earth, 1972.

————. *The Place No One Knew: Glen Canyon on the Colorado.* San Francisco: Sierra Club, 1968.

————. *The Sierra Club Wilderness Handbook.* New York: Ballantine Books, 1967.

Brower, David, and Robert Moses. "The Conservation Issue: Sound, Fury and Substance." *The Conservationist,* 27 (February-March 1973), 14-16.

Carson, Rachel. *Silent Spring.* Boston: Houghton Mifflin, 1962.

"A Conservationist Speaks His Mind." *U.S. News and World Report,* 71 (July 5, 1971), 64-5.

Davies, Lawrence E. "Naturalists Get a Political Arm." *New York Times,* September 17, 1969, p. 21.

————. "Sierra Club Head Asks Leave in Bid to Oust Critics." *New York Times,* February 8, 1969, p. 15.

"Executive Director of the Sierra Club Is Curbed by Board." *New York Times,* February 9, 1969, p. 65.

Hill, Gladwin. "Brower Quitting: Plans New Organziation." *New York Times,* May 4, 1969, p. 30.

————. "Conservatives Win Sierra Club Vote: Director May Be Ousted." *New York Times,* April 17, 1969, p. 94.

————. "Sierra Club Sending out Ballots for a Vote Vital to Its Future." *New York Times,* March 14, 1969, p. 20.

Jones, Robert A. "Fratricide in the Sierra Club." *The Nation,* 208 (May 5, 1969), 567-70.

McPhee, John. *Encounters with the Archdruid.* New York: Farrar, Straus and Giroux, 1971.

Peterson, Harold. "Brower Power Awaits the Verdict." *Sports Illustrated,* 30 (April 14, 1969), 36-8, 41-3.

"Sierra Club Chief Is Granted Leave." *New York Times,* February 10, 1969, p. 39.

Stegner, Wallace, Ed. *This Is Dinosaur: Echo Park Country and Its Magic Rivers.* New York: Knopf, 1955.

Strong, Douglas H. "The Sierra Club — A History: Part I: Origins and Outings." *Sierra: The Sierra Club Bulletin,* 62 (October 1977), 10-14.

————. "The Sierra Club — A History: Part II: Conservation." *Sierra: The Sierra Club Bulletin,* 62 (November/December 1977), 16-20.

Thurber, Scott. "Conservation Comes of Age." *The Nation,* 204 (February 27, 1967), 272-75.

"Using Less." *The New Yorker,* 49 (October 22, 1973), 35-6.

CHAPTER 14
Garrett Hardin and Overpopulation:
Lifeboats vs. Mountain Climbers

Bikales, Gerda. "Immigration Policy: The New Environmental Battlefield." *National Parks and Conservation Magazine.* 51 (December 1977), 13-16.

Commoner, Barry. *The Closing Circle.* New York: Knopf, 1971.

————. *The Poverty of Power: Energy and the Economic Crisis.* New York: Knopf, 1976.

Cousins, Norman. " 'Lifeboat Ethics.' " *Saturday Review,* 3 (October 18, 1975), 4.

————. "Of Life and Lifeboats." *Saturday Review,* 2 (March 8, 1975), 4.

Crowe, Beryl L. "The Tragedy of the Commons Revisited." *Science,* 166 (November 28, 1969), 1103-7.

De Voss, David. "What Ever Happened to California?" *Time* 110 (July 18, 1977), 22-23.

Ehrlich, Paul R. *The Population Bomb.* 2nd. ed. New York: Ballantine, 1971.

————, and Anne H. Ehrlich. *The End of Affluence.* New York: Ballantine, 1974.

————; Anne H. Ehrlich; and John P. Holdren. *Ecoscience: Population, Resources, Environment.* San Francisco: W. H. Freeman, 1977.

Elliott, Charles. *Patterns of Poverty in the Third World.* New York: Praeger, 1975.

Hardin, Garrett. *Exploring New Ethics for Survival: The Voyage of the Spaceship Beagle.* New York: Viking, 1972.

————. "Gregg's Law." *BioScience,* 25 (July 1975), 415.

————. *The Limits of Altruism.* Bloomington: Indiana University Press, 1977.

————. "Living on a Lifeboat." *BioScience,* 24 (October 1974), 561-8.

————. *Nature and Man's Fate.* New York: Rinehart, 1959.

————. *Stalking the Wild Taboo.* Los Altos, California: William Kaufman, 1973.

————. "The Tragedy of the Commons." *Science,* 162 (December 13, 1968), 1243-8.

————, Ed. *Population, Evolution, and Birth Control.* 2nd ed. San Francisco: W. H. Freeman, 1969.

————, and John Baden, Eds. *Managing the Commons.* San Francisco: W. H. Freeman, 1977.

"Letters." *BioScience,* 25 (May 1975), 292.

McMahon, John J. "Garrett Hardin and the Search for Ecological Morality." *The Living Wilderness,* 37 (Spring 1973), 22-9.

Miller, Ralph. "Stalking the Stalker of the Wild Taboo: A Profile of Garrett Hardin." *Equilibrium,* 1 (July 1973), 30-3.

Mills, Stephanie. "The Ehrlichs Talk: Equity and Apocalypse." *Not Man Apart,* 7 (October 1977), 2-4.

Murdock, William W., and Allan Oaten. "Population and Food: Metaphors and the Reality." *BioScience,* 25 (September 1975), 561-7.

Ogilvy, Stewart. "Population Strategy: Toward a New Ethic of Numbers." *Not Man Apart,* 7 (Mid-December 1977), 2-4.

Paddock, William, and Paul Paddock. *Famine, 1975!* Boston: Little, Brown, 1967.

Piotrow, Phyllis Tilson. *World Population Crisis: The United States Response.* New York: Praeger, 1973.

CHAPTER 15
Working From Within: Stewart Udall
Finds Conservation Good Politics

Callison, Charles H. "Stewart L. Udall: Audubon Medalist—1967." *Audubon,* 70 (January 1968), 25.

Clawson, Marion. *Uncle Sam's Acres.* New York: Dodd, Mead, 1951.

Conconi, Charles. "There are No Technological Solutions: An Interview with Stewart L. Udall." *The Living Wilderness,* 39 (July 1975), 17-20.

————; David Osterhout, and Stewart Udall. *The Energy Balloon.* McGraw-Hill, 1974.

"Conservation's Future." *The New Republic,* 160 (January 4, 1969), 12-13.

"Editorial: Brass Tacks Conservation." *American Forests,* 69 (March 1963), 9, 51.

Fifer, Orien W., Jr. "First Arizonan in Cabinet: Pioneering Tradition for Bearers of Udall Name." Phoenix *Arizona Republic,* February 18, 1962, pp. 1-A, 12-A.

————. "Stewart Udall Leader As Boy." Phoenix *Arizona Republic,* February 19, 1962, pp. 1, 14.

————. "Stewart Udall Thrives in Hectic Washington." Phoenix *Arizona Republic,* February 20, 1962, pp. 1, 16.

————. "Udall's Confidence, Drive Guide Him in Tasks Today." Phoenix *Arizona Republic,* February 21, 1962, pp. 15, 17.

"Kennedy's Cabinet: New 'Team': Brainy, Young, Mid-Road." *U.S. News and World Report,* 49 (December 26, 1960), 32-33, 36.

"LBJ Gives Udall Wider Role." *Business Week,* No. 1857 (April 3, 1965), 98-100, 105, 107.

O'Reilly, John. "Udall at the Bridge." *Sports Illustrated,* 14 (May 15, 1961), 26-27.

Peffer, E. Louise. *The Closing of the Public Domain: Disposal and Reservation Policies, 1900-50.* Stanford: Stanford University Press, 1951.

Prokop, John. "Well Done, Mr. Secretary!" *American Forests,* 69 (March 1963), 8, 41-42, 44.

Robbins, Roy M. *Our Landed Heritage: The Public Domain, 1776-1970.* 2nd. rev. ed. Lincoln: University of Nebraska Press, 1976.

"Stewart Udall Still Active in Private Life." *Houston Post,* September 1, 1977, p. 2 N.

"Tackling the Environment." *Time,* 93 (February 7, 1969), 18.

Udall, Stewart. "Call Them Human Life Refuges." *Audubon,* 70 (January 1968), 26, 28, 30.

————. "The Last Traffic Jam: Too Many Cars, Too Little Oil" *The Atlantic Monthly,* 230 (October 1972), 72-74, 76.

————. "The Mining Law of 1872 Must Be Scrapped." *National Wildlife,* 8 (June 1970), 9-11.

————. *1976: Agenda for Tomorrow.* New York: Harcourt, Brace and World, 1968.

————. *The Quiet Crisis.* New York: Holt, Rinehart and Winston, 1963.

"Udall's Last Laugh." *The New Republic,* 160 (February 1, 1969), 10.

"Udall's Last Stand." *The Nation,* 208 (February 10, 1969), 164-65.

Watkins, T. H., and Charles S. Watson, Jr. *The Land No One Knows: America and the Public Domain.* San Francisco: Sierra Club, 1975.

CHAPTER 16
Working From Without: Edward Abbey,
Part Zorro, Part Ezekiel

Abbey, Edward. *Appalachian Wilderness: The Great Smokey Mountains.* New York: E. P. Dutton, 1973.

―――――. *Black Sun: A Novel.* New York: Simon and Schuster, 1971.

―――――. *The Brave Cowboy: An Old Tale in a New Time.* New York: Dodd, Mead, 1956.

―――――. *Cactus Country.* New York: Time-Life Books, 1973.

―――――. *Desert Solitaire: A Season in the Wilderness.* New York: McGraw-Hill, 1968.

―――――. *Fire on the Mountain.* New York: The Dial Press, 1962.

―――――. "God Bless America. Let's Save Some of It." *High Country News* (Lander, Wyoming), May 19, 1978, pp. 1, 4-5.

―――――. *Jonathan Troy.* New York: Dodd, Mead, 1954.

―――――. *The Journey Home: Some Words in Defense of the American West.* New York: E. P. Dutton, 1977.

―――――. "Joy, Shipmates, Joy!: Survival with Honor in the Rocky Mountain West." *High Country News* (Lander, Wyoming), September 24, 1976, pp. 1, 4-5.

―――――. "Let Us Now Praise Mountains Lions." *Life,* 68 (March 13, 1970), 52B-53B, 54-58.

————. "Living on the Last Whole Earth." *Natural History,* 80 (November 1971), 84-88.

————. *The Monkey Wrench Gang.* Philadelphia: J. B. Lippincott, 1975.

————. "On Nature, the Modern Temper, and the Southwest: An Interview with Joseph Wood Krutch." *Sage,* 2 (Spring 1968), 13-21.

————. "The Right to Arms." *Playboy: Entertainment for Men,* 24 (January 1977), 41-42.

————. *Slickrock: The Canyon Country of Southeast Utah.* San Francisco: Sierra Club, 1971.

————. "The West's Land of Surprises, Some Terrible." *Harper's,* 233 (December 1966), 98-107.

————. "White Water Ramblers." *Playboy: Entertainment for Men,* 24 (August 1977), 88-90, 114, 167, 172, 174-75.

————, and John Blaustein. *The Hidden Canyon: A River Journey.* New York: Penguin, 1977.

Baker, John F. "Edward Abbey." *Publishers Weekly,* 208 (September 8, 1975), 6-7.

Barker, Larry. "Edward Abbey Doesn't Really Want to Blow up the Glen Canyon Dam." *The New Mexico Independent,* 80 (March 26, 1976), 6, 8.

Hamilton, Bruce. "Edward Abbey: Druid of the Arches." *High Country News* (Lander, Wyoming), December 31, 1976, pp. 1, 6, 7.

McCann, Garth. *Edward Abbey.* Boise, Idaho: Boise State University Western Writers Series, 1977.

McLellan, Jack. "Kaiparowits: Southern Utah at the Crossroads." *Sierra Club Bulletin,* 60 (August-September 1975), 6-8, 26-27.

Parfit, Michael. "Showdown at Kaiparowits." *New Times,* 6 (April 2, 1976), 46-53.

Powell, Lawrence Clark. "A Singular Ranger." *Westways,* 66 (March 1974), 32-35, 64-65.

"Redford Burned in Effigy for Opposing Power Plant." *New York Times,* April 19, 1976, p. 17.

Sibley, George. "The Desert Empire." *Harper's,* 255 (October 1977), 49-56, 61-68.

CHAPTER 17
Discovering Ourselves

Bigart, Robert, Ed. *Environmental Pollution in Montana.* Missoula, Montana: Mountain Press Publishing Company, 1972.

Blumberg, Stanley A., and Gwinn Owens. *Energy and Conflict: The Life and Times of Edward Teller.* New York: Putnam, 1976.

Bradley, Richard C. *The Costs of Urban Growth.* Colorado Springs, Colorado: Pikes Peak Area Council of Governments, 1973.

Browning, Frank. *The Vanishing Land: Corporate Theft of America's Soil.* New York: Harper and Row, 1975.

Commoner, Barry. *The Poverty of Power.* New York: Knopf, 1976.

Gordon, Suzanne. *Black Mesa: The Angel of Death.* New York: John Day Company, 1973.

Lewallen, John, and James Robertson. *The Grass Roots Primer.* Sierra Club, 1975.

Mitchell, John G. *Losing Ground.* San Francisco: Sierra Club, 1975.

Schell, Orville. *The Town That Fought to Save Itself.* New York: Pantheon Books, 1976.

Schneider, Stephen H. *The Genesis Strategy.* New York: Plenum Press, 1976.

Schumacher, E. F. *Small is Beautiful.* New York: Harper and Row, 1973.

Udall, Stewart. *1976: Agenda for Tommorow*. New York: Harcourt, Brace and World, 1968.

Waters, Frank. *To Possess the Land*. Chicago: The Swallow Press, 1973.

Worster, Donald. *Nature's Economy: The Roots of Ecology*. San Francisco: Sierra Club, 1977.

Young, Louise B. *Power over People*. New York: Oxford University Press, 1973.

Index

239

Colorado, 11,15, 20, 26, 27, 67, 76-78, 114, 207.
Colorado Plateau, 173, 189.
Colorado River, 23, 24, 25, 100, 180, 181, 185.
Columbia River,1, 2, 147.
Columbia University, 134, 138.
Law School, 142, 144.
Columbus, Christopher, 2, 3
Committee on Interior and Insular Affairs, 178.
Commoner, Barry, 169.
Conant, James Bryant, 107.
Concord, Massachussetts, 34, 36.
Concord River, 5.
Coney Island, 138.
Congress, U.S., 20-21, 26, 40-41, 47, 49, 53-55, 60, 62, 64, 68, 69, 109, 115, 127, 128, 133, 146, 175, 176, 178, 195.
Creates Division of Forestry in Dept. of Agriculture, 47.
Library of, 50.
Passes comprehensive National Parks Bill, 43.
Passes Wilderness Act of 1964, 128.
Congressmen, 12, 22, 40, 61, 63-64, 67, 69, 111, 156, 179, 182, 186, 194, 206.
Cramton, Louis Convers, 69.
Crockett, David (Tenn. State Leg.), 5.
Kent, William, 62, 64, 68.
LaFollette, Robert, 175.
Marsh, George P, 5.
Neuberger, Richard L., 110.
Saylor, John P., 174.
Stafford, William, 66.
Western, 26, 52, 110.
Udall, Morris, 174.
Udall, Stewart, 178.
Connecticut, 128, 136.
Continental Divide, 72, 76.
Contra Costa County, California, 40.
Coolidge, Calvin, 177.
Cope, Edward Drinker, 14.
Cornell University, 50.
Cosmopolitan Magazine, 85.
Cotton, Ellen, 16-17.
The Course of Empire, 107.
Cousins, Norman, 162, 169.
Cramton, Louis C., 69.
Crash of 1929 (stock market), 144.
Cree Tribe, 118.
Cripple Creek, Colorado, 11.
Crockett, David, 5.
The Crooked Mile, 106.

Czar of Russia, 11.
Dakotas, the, 8.
Dallas, Texas, 164.
Dannen, Kent, 79.
Darwin, Charles, 15.
Defenders of Wildlife, 136.
Democratic National Convention, 178.
Depression, the, 56, 103, 134, 145, 165, 174, 190.
Desert Telegraph, 25, 173.
Desert Solitaire: A Season in the Wilderness, 194-195, 196.
The Desert Year, 137.
Detroit, Michigan, 174.
"Devil's Domain," 131-132.
DeVoto, Avis, 108.
DeVoto, Bernard, 9, 104 (photograph), 105-111, 137, 144.
Diablo Canyon, 153.
Dickinson, Emily, 90.
Dinosaur National Monument, 67, 155-156.
Disney, Walt
Disneyland, 194.
Productions, 148.
District of Columbia Stadium (Robert Kennedy Stadium), 182.
Dobie, J. Frank, 5, 15, 125.
Dodd, Mead Publishing Co., 192.
Douglas, Kirk, 193.
Douglas, William O., 127, 140 (photograph), 141-149, 182, 187.
Dryptosaurus, 14.
Dunbar, Scotland, 31.
Dust Bowl, 22, 174.
Dutton, E.P., publishing company, 196.

Earth Horizon, 84.
East, the, 5-6, 7, 8, 9, 15, 16, 20, 21, 35, 40, 41, 69, 73, 79, 108, 144, 154, 192.
Echo Park Dam, 67.
Eco-raiders, 185.
Eden, 9, 154.
Edinburgh, University of, 191.
Edward Abbey, 191.
Ehrlich, Paul, 157, 168, 170.
Eisley, Loren, 76.
Eisenhower, Dwight D., 67, 177.
El Dorado, 2, 19.
Eliot, George, 168.
The Elk of North America, 124.
Ellis Island, 6.
Emerson, Ralph Waldo, 3, 5, 32, 34-37, 90.
Emma Dean, flagship, 25.

2970